Good-Night Vienna

An Operetta

Eric Maschwitz

A SAMUEL FRENCH ACTING EDITION

SAMUEL FRENCH

FOUNDED 1830

SAMUELFRENCH-LONDON.CO.UK
SAMUELFRENCH.COM

FOR AMATEUR PRODUCTION ENQUIRIES

UNITED KINGDOM AND WORLD
EXCLUDING NORTH AMERICA
plays@SamuelFrench-London.co.uk
020 7255 4302/01

Each title is subject to availability from Samuel French,

depending upon country of performance.

CHARACTERS

(in the order of their appearance)

FRIEDL
VICKI   } assistants in the Flower Shop

CILLI, the delivery girl

LEA STEINMETZ
ILENA KRAUSS } customers

LT ERNST
LT JOHANN
COUNT MAX SCHMETTOFF } officers of the Imperial Guard

GRETA, owner of the Flower Shop

HANS, a former employee

PRINCE SCHMETTOFF, father of Count Max

ORDERLY

THE COUNTESS HELGA

THE BARONESS, friend of the Prince

WILHELM, major-domo to the Prince

AN ELDERLY DIPLOMAT

HIS PARTNER

FRAULEIN GUMP, from the kennels

HERR GRUH, a wealthy profiteer

MITZI, his lady friend

FRAU GRUH, his wife

NIKI, her gigolo

SHOP GIRLS, OFFICERS OF THE IMPERIAL GUARD, GUESTS AT THE SCHMETTOFF PALACE, WAITRESSES, WAITERS AND CLIENTS AT "THE HOUSE IN THE TREES", etc.

SYNOPSIS OF SCENES

ACT I
A Flower Shop in Vienna (June 1914)

ACT II
The Terrace of the Schmettoff Palace (July 1914)

ACT III
The House in the Trees (after the war)

MUSIC

ACT I

No.

	Overture	
1	"Love's Bouquet"	FRIEDL, VICKI *and* GIRLS
2	"There's No-One Buys Flowers For Me"	CILLI *and* GIRLS
3	"Marching Song of the Guard"	MAX, JOHANN, ERNST, OFFICERS *and* GIRLS
3a	Reprise (Exit)	OFFICERS *and* GIRLS
4	"It's Such a Tricky Thing, This Love"	HANS *and* CILLI
4a	Exit of Hans and Cilli	
5	"My Pretty Flowers"	GRETA *and* MAX
6	"Wine, Women and War"	MAX, JOHANN *and* ERNST, OFFICERS *and* GIRLS
7	"Good-Night Vienna"	MAX, GRETA *and* COMPANY
7a	Melos: Entrance of Helga	
8	Finale	GRETA *and* COMPANY

ACT II

9	"Vienna Waltz Ballet"	CHORUS *and* DANCERS
9a	Exit Music	
10	"Dear Little Waltz"	ERNST, JOHANN, VICKI, FRIEDL *and* CHORUS
11	"When a Woman Wears a Ring"	HELGA
12	"A Little Delicatessen For Two"	HANS *and* CILLI
13	Melos: Entrance of Greta and betrothal scene	
14	"Just Heaven"	MAX *and* GRETA
15	Melos: Declaration of War	
16	Melos: Finale	

ACT III

17	"Come to the House in the Trees"	ERNST, JOHANN *and* CHORUS
18	"You Can Take Me Out To Supper"	CILLI *and* COMPANY
19	"No More"	MAX
20	Melos: Arrival of the Guests	
21	Speciality Ballet: "Tyrolean Life"	

ACT I

OVERTURE

Scene—*The Interior of a Flower Shop in Vienna, late in the afternoon of 28th June 1914.*

*The premises are prettily decorated in a style to match the fairy-tale nature of the operetta as well as the flowers that are everywhere in profusion. Up c is the shop-window, a gauze lettered in reverse with the name of the establishment—"*blumenparadies*". Through the gauze can be seen the backcloth of a narrow, very picturesque street.*

Below the window is a rostrum with entrances L and R which is approached by shallow carpeted steps, c. Below the line of the steps L and R are two entrance archways separated by an attractive counter carrying a rich display of summer blossoms. Downstage L of c is a chaise longue for the accommodation of customers. Downstage R is a round table on which are order books, spools of coloured ribbon, and material for writing greeting-cards.

When the Curtain *rises,* Shop Girls *are making up orders and arranging flowers. As they work they sing and dance. Throughout the Act,* Passers-by *of various types and ages may be seen beyond the window, to add to the movement and costume-colour of the action, but this effect should be used discreetly and not become distracting or repetitive.*

<table>
<tr><td colspan="2" align="center">"LOVE'S BOUQUET"</td><td align="right">No. 1</td></tr>
</table>

Girls.	All the flowers in Vienna gay,
	Here you'll find every day—
	Orchids and lilies and roses,
	Yet there is only a kiss to pay.
	Golden hours in Vienna gay,
	Live, laugh, love
	While you may.
	Oh, do not delay,
	Sweetest flowers fade with hours.
	We've found out the way
	To make love's bouquet!
Friedl.	These are the flowers for Fritzi.
Vicki.	For the fairest one on his list.
Friedl.	These are from Otto to Mitzi.
Vicki.	She is his Love-in-a-mist.
Girls.	Our trade is the flower trade,
	But the love trade is the root of our calling.
	Our game is the flower game,

	And the love game of all the world.

	Ah—!
VICKI.	Sweet are the blossoms we send her,
	Bringing the hopes of her lover,
	Pleading his passion without any words—
	Such is the way of love.
GIRLS.	Our trade is the flower trade,
	But the love trade is the root of our calling.
	Our game is the flower game,
	And the love game of all the world.

All the flowers in Vienna gay,
Here you'll find every day—
Orchids and lilies and roses,
Yet there is only a kiss to pay.
Golden hours in Vienna gay,
Live, laugh, love
While you may.
Oh, do not delay,
Sweetest flowers fade with hours.
We've found out the way
To make love's bouquet.

(When the music is finished there is a piercing feminine scream from off up L. CILLI *enters up* L. *She is an attractive, if "well-built", young person in the uniform and peaked cap of a delivery girl. She has more or less to feel her way since someone has crammed over her head a deep cardboard box from which trail some rather damaged carnations)*

ALL. Cilli! *(They all laugh)*

*(*VICKI *and* FRIEDL *run to Cilli's rescue as she misses her foothold and almost tumbles down the steps* C)

CILLI *(muffled)* Help!

*(*VICKI *removes the box, disclosing* CILLI'S *indignant expression)*

VICKI. Cilli, whatever happened?
CILLI *(tremulously)* I took Lea Steinmetz's order for carnations to the Operetta Theatre and look what she did with 'em!

(Everyone laughs. At that moment LEA STEINMETZ *enters from up* L. *She is a tall, temperamental blonde and flourishes a sunshade furiously)*

LEA. Where is that girl? Where *is* the little monster? *(She catches sight of the cowering Cilli)* Ah, *there* you are! *(She advances threateningly)*
VICKI *(interposing deftly)* Miss Steinmetz seems to be upset . . .
LEA. *Seems* to be? Miss Steinmetz *is* upset!
VICKI. There must be some mistake. We sent you ten dozen carnations.
LEA *(grimly)* You did . . . and whose name was on the card?

FRIEDL (*consulting an order-book*) They were from Captain Klotz of the Hussars.

LEA (*scornfully*) From Klotz? From *that* corsetted little weasel? And *what* has happened to my regular delivery of roses?

VICKI }
FRIEDL } (*together; pretending to be mystified*) Roses, mam'oiselle?

(*The* GIRLS *exchange amused glances and shrug their shoulders*)

LEA. Yes—roses! (*She stamps her foot angrily*)

(ILENA KRAUSS *enters up* L. *She is a tall, handsome brunette. She, too, flourishes a parasol and glares around with indignation*)

FRIEDL (*aside to Vicki*) Look out, here's another contented customer!

ILENA (*advancing down the steps to Cilli*) Are you the manager?

CILLI. Me? No, I'm the delivery girl.

VICKI. Excuse me, Miss Krauss, but we already have a customer. (*She indicates Lea*)

ILENA (*to Vicki*) I insist on an explanation.

LEA (*to Friedl*) I demand an answer. Where are my flowers?

ILENA. What has happened to *my* usual order?

BOTH (*together*) From Count Schmettoff.

(*The two tigresses "do a take" and turn on each other*)

LEA (*to Ilena*) And what is Count Max to *you?*

ILENA (*with an elaborate shrug*) Oh, nothing. He's merely been sending me flowers every month for the past year!

LEA. Impossible. He sends flowers to *me* every month.

ILENA. I hardly think so. You see, *I* am the Count's special friend!

LEA. I doubt whether you could have been more *special* than me.

ILENA (*raising her parasol*) How dare you?

LEA (*raising her parasol*) And how dare *you?*

VICKI (*intervening*) I'm very sorry, ladies, but both orders were cancelled a month ago! (*She closes the order-book*)

LEA }
ILENA } (*together; indignantly*) Cancelled?

VICKI (*nodding*) Yes! And no renewal!

LEA. I'll see Max about this!

ILENA. See him? I'll murder him.

LEA (*with false tenderness*) I think he's treated you abominably!

ILENA. Poor *you!* I can't think how you can stand it.

LEA. Come and have a drink, dear.

ILENA. A good idea. The brandies are on *me!*

(*Exit* LEA *and* ILENA *up* L, *arm in arm*)

FRIEDL. Well, did you ever? That was a quick change!

VICKI. Maybe, but (*she turns up to the window*) just wait and see!

(EVERYONE *turns up to the window.* LEA *and* ILENA *cross to* R *outside the window, talking angrily. We cannot hear what they are saying but as they disappear* R *a furious parasol battle develops between them.* EVERYONE *on stage doubles up with laughter*)

CILLI. That Count Max certainly gets around!

VICKI. And how about *you* "getting around", my girl—and finishing the deliveries?

CILLI (*disconsolately*) I'm fed up with taking flowers to other women.

FRIEDL. Want to be at the receiving end for a change?

"THERE'S NO-ONE BUYS FLOWERS FOR ME" No. 2

CILLI (*speaking over the music*). Well, why not? I'm young, I'm healthy and I have the rudest ideas.

(*She sings*) Men may buy a bouquet
      For any sweetie they see,
      When they buy a bouquet
      I must deliver it free!
      Mein Gott, as I'm trudging the sidewalks of town
      Those other girls' roses are weighing me down!

      There's no-one buys flowers for me
      Not a He thinks of me.
      There's no-one builds bowers for me
      Though I'm footloose and free.
      When once I believed an admirer I'd got
      He seemed to react as though passion was hot.
      But he sent me a cactus—and that was the lot!
      For no-one buys flowers for me.

GIRLS.   You'd do better, Cilli,
      If you were frail and frilly,
      The type like an orchid
      That lovers adore.
      A man's afraid to tussle
      With maidens made of muscle
      For fear he'll end up on the floor!

CILLI.   Well, no-one buys flowers for me
      I'm a She all at sea.
      There's no-one braves showers for me
      Just to see if I'm free.
      It might be expensive to take me to lunch
      Though I'm on a diet I do like to munch,
      Still daisies are cheap now at fourpence a bunch,
      Yet no-one buys flowers for me!

(*A Dance Chorus follows during which the* GIRLS *load Cilli with parcels until she is hardly visible.* CILLI *peers over the load to sing a last refrain*)

> I may not be svelte
> (That's the français for slim)
> And pop on a belt just to keep myself trim,
> But oh, when I melt
> There'll be plenty for him,
> The man who buys flowers for me!

(*As the music ends the* GIRLS *all laugh*)

CILLI. What's so funny about it all?

FRIEDL. You had your big chance, Cilli, but you let him go!

CILLI (*bitterly*) My big chance? Big? That miserable little Hansi? I did my best to be nice to him—and what did the little runt do? Sneaked out of town and left me holding his job!

(*Carrying her parcels* CILLI *staggers off up* L, *guided by the* GIRLS *who tease her as she goes. Some of them follow her off*)

VICKI (*to the others who remain*) Come along, now. (*She claps her hands commandingly*) We're not finished yet!

(*All the* GIRLS *except Friedl and Vicki exit* R *and* L *about their business.* VICKI *sits at the table down* R *and studies an order-book, a pencil to her lips*)

FRIEDL (*coming down to Vicki*) Cilli was right, you know. Count Max is a real ball of fire!

VICKI (*looking up doubtfully*) Yes, I suppose so . . .

FRIEDL. Think what he's done for the business. Why, he's practically turned this place into a regimental headquarters. (*Ecstatically*) Oh, those *darling* officers!

VICKI (*slyly, rising*) Such as Lieutenant Ernst?

FRIEDL. What of it? *You* don't seem to be exactly bored by Lieutenant Johann!

VICKI. Friedl, it's all very well for you and me—we can have a little romance and no bones broken! (*She pauses*) But I'm worried about Greta . . .

FRIEDL (*with a shrug*) Greta? She's doing fine. She's got this shop and the Count as well!

VICKI (*a little scornfully*) Major the Honourable Max Schmettoff, the son of the Court Chamberlain, and a village girl from Grinzing who runs a flower shop . . . ?

FRIEDL. He's crazy about her. You heard those two man-eaters just now. Since he met Greta, he hasn't had a thought for anyone else.

VICKI (*doubtfully*) You know what men can be.

"MARCHING SONG OF THE GUARD"   No. 3

(Starting very quietly, music is heard—as though in the distance)

FRIEDL *(speaking over the music)* You bet I do . . . and here they come to prove it!

OFFICERS *(singing, as though in the distance, off R)*
> We are the regiment of devil-may-cares,
> When in attack we are a crack brigade,
> Never afraid!

VICKI *(speaking over the singing)* Back from manœuvres . . .

FRIEDL *(speaking over the singing)* And not a moment too soon!

(The singing comes nearer)

OFFICERS *(off R)*
> If to be brave is wealth, we're millionaires.
> We pay our debts with bayonets,
> Oh! war is a wonderful trade.

(OFFICERS of the Imperial Guard appear above the window up R. GIRLS enter excitedly, L and R, waving to them. The OFFICERS swagger across to L in informal order. Bringing up the rear are LT ERNST, LT JOHANN and MAJOR SCHMETTOFF—Count MAX Schmettoff)

> When in the days of peace we've nothing to do,
> A handsome lot, we're really not above
> Falling in love.

(The OFFICERS enter the shop from up L. The GIRLS eagerly flock to meet them)

> But when the trumpets make a hullabaloo,
> What are we longing for?
> Just war!

(As the music continues, the GIRLS surround the Officers admiringly)

MAX.   Here the regiment comes,
> The echoes ringing as they march along
> To the beat of the drums,
> While ev'ry man is joining in the song.
>
> We are the regiment of devil-may-cares,
> When in attack we are a crack brigade,
> Never afraid!
> If to be brave is wealth, we're millionaires.
> We pay our debts with bayonets,
> Oh! war is a wonderful trade.
> When in the days of peace we've nothing to do,
> A handsome lot, we're really not above
> Falling in love.

But when the trumpets make a hullabaloo,
What are we longing for?
Just war!

Hark, along the street
The people cheer them as they march away.
Hark, the tramp of their feet
While every voice is singing loud and gay:
OFFICERS *and* GIRLS.
We are the regiment of devil-may-cares,
When in attack we are a crack brigade,
Never afraid!
If to be brave is wealth, we're millionaires.
We pay our debts with bayonets,
Oh! war is a wonderful trade.
When in the days of peace we've nothing to do,
A handsome lot, we're really not above
Falling in love.
But when the trumpets make a hullabaloo,
What are we longing for?
Just war!
War!
Just war!

VICKI. Johann, my angel! (*She embraces him*)
ERNST. Friedl, my beloved pet! (*He embraces her*)
MAX (*amused*) And what about *me?*
ERNST. You, Max? You don't deserve anything.
JOHANN (*feelingly*) Ten miles—and not a "march at ease" the whole way!

(*The* GIRLS *groan sympathetically*)

The Major, of course, rides a horse!
VICKI. Oh! I *do* call that mean!
FRIEDL. I don't see why you have to have these silly manœuvres.
MAX. Colonel's orders, my dear. Stiffen up training all round—ready for August.
VICKI. Why August? There isn't going to be a war?
MAX. A war? Good Heavens, no. Just another General Inspection—with his Imperial Majesty in a carriage—and a silver cross for anyone who's lucky!

(EVERYONE *laughs*)

(*Looking round*) Where's Greta?
VICKI. Don't say you've forgotten . . . it's Tuesday. Greta has her singing lesson.
MAX (*without enthusiasm*) Don't tell me she's keeping up that nonsense still?
VICKI. Nonsense! The Professor says she has a wonderful voice . . .

Friedl (*to Ernst, mischievously*) A girl who loses her heart to a soldier *needs* a second string—just in case!

(Ernst *makes a grab at her. Turning up stage to avoid him* Friedl *sees* Greta *enter* R, *in the street*)

Ssh! Here she comes. (*To Max*) Get out of sight . . . give her a surprise.

(Max *ducks out of sight as* Greta *enters up* L. *She is a pretty young girl dressed in a becoming street costume. She is gaily humming a Strauss waltz*)

We-ell, *you* sound very happy.
Greta. Yes, I *am* very happy.
Vicki. Anything special?
Greta (*producing a telegram, which she shows to Vicki*) This telegram, Vicki. It came this afternoon while I was at my lesson. The Professor wrote to his cousin in Paris about me and now—guess what—they've offered me a small part in the Opera!

(*The* Girls *react excitedly.* Vicki *seizes the telegram and studies it*)

Friedl. Paris? How wonderful! Fancy being able to go to Paris!
Vicki. She hasn't said she's going yet. (*She glances at Max*) Do you want to go, Greta?
Max (*stepping forward*) Yes, do you want to go?
Greta (*surprised and delighted*) Max!
Max. Sweetheart, you haven't answered my question.
Greta (*after a hesitation*) Of course I'm not going. (*She holds out her hands to Max*)

(Max *takes her in his arms and kisses her*)

(*Breaking away; teasingly*) Still, it *was* rather nice to have been asked. And Paris . . . with all those charming Frenchmen, and the parties in Monmartre.
Max. To blazes with Monmartre! *I'm* going to give a party right here in Vienna, tonight!

(Everyone *cheers*)

You're all invited—on one condition, though.

(*There are murmurs of disappointment*)

No Frenchmen!

(Everyone *laughs*)

We'll go to the House in the Trees.

(*The suggestion is greeted with enthusiasm*)

Greta. That wonderful music. And the nightingales singing in the forest.

MAX. I'll order a special choir of nightingales, and if they don't sing properly we'll have their tongues for supper!

(EVERYONE *laughs*)

GRETA (*taking Max's hand*) You have the loveliest ideas.

JOHANN. And *I* have a lovely idea, too. Junior officers' privilege this time—to provide the young ladies with a glass of wine before they close the shop?

MAX. Brilliant!

ERNST. A stroke of genius!

OFFICERS. Hear! Hear! (*They embrace the Girls*)

JOHANN (*to Greta*) Might we have some assistance in getting in the supplies?

GRETA (*pretending to be serious*) I shall have to think about that . . .

GIRLS. Oh, *please?*

GRETA (*appearing to relent*) Very well . . . be off, the lot of you. I'll stay and keep an eye on things.

MAX (*fondly*) And so will I!

GRETA (*shaking her head*) No, Max, I need *you* to keep an eye on the *girls* and see that they return to duty.

MAX. As your Highness commands. (*In very military fashion*) Officers attached to the Imperial Guard, 'shun!

(*The* OFFICERS *spring to attention*)

Ladies attached to the officers attached to the Imperial Guard, 'shun!

(*The* GIRLS *obey*)

Right—dress!

(*Sharing the joke, everyone shuffles about, getting into line*)

About—turn!

(EVERYONE *turns to face up stage.* MAX *siezes the opportunity of taking Greta in his arms and kissing her. After a few seconds, puzzled by the silence, the* OFFICERS *and* GIRLS *begin to turn round*)

ALL (*spotting Max and Greta kissing*) Hey!

MAX (*releasing Greta and laughing*) Left—turn!

(*The* OFFICERS *and* GIRLS *turn to face* L *stage*)

To fetch supplies,—quick—march!

REPRISE—"MARCHING SONG"—EXIT   No. 3a

OFFICERS *and* GIRLS.

We
They are the regiment of devil-may-cares,
When in attack we are a crack brigade,
Never afraid!

If to be brave is wealth, we're millionaires.
We pay our debts with bayonets,
Oh! war is a wonderful trade.
When in the days of peace we've nothing to do,
A handsome lot, we're really not above
Falling in love.
But when the trumpets make a hullabaloo,
What are we longing for?
Just war!

(*Except for Greta,* Everyone *marches off* L. Max *waves to Greta as he leaves the stage last. The singing dies into the distance.* Cilli *enters* R. *Now empty-handed, having delivered her parcels, she is weary and woe-begone*)

Cilli (*bitterly, as the singing dies*) So they're back . . . and at it again!
Greta. Poor Cilli. You've had a hard day.
Cilli. My feet are on fire. Talk about fried soles!
Greta. Cheer up. We'll see you get something to revive you when the party begins!

(Cilli *and* Greta *begin to exit, down* R)

Cilli (*as she goes*) It's all very well for *you* to be cheerful, Miss Greta, but what's a party without a *man!*

(*They exit. After a short pause,* Hans *enters up* L. *He is a small man, dressed in the uniform of a private in the Imperial Guard, weighed down by his pack, haversack, kit-bag, cartridge belt and other assorted items of equipment. Nevertheless, he sings jauntily to himself as he arrives*)

Hans (*singing sotto voce, unaccompanied*)
We are the regiment of devil-may-cares,
When in attack we are a crack brigade,
Never afraid!

(*Seeing the shop deserted, he tiptoes down the steps, looking to* R *and* L. *Suddenly he hears* Cilli's *voice, and ducks out of sight behind the chaise-longue*)

Cilli (*off* R) Don't you worry, Miss Greta. I'll keep an eye on the shop for you . . . (*she enters* R) as long as I can do it *sitting down.* (*She limps towards the chaise-longue*)
Hans (*jumping up with proudly outstretched arms, and letting his equipment drop with a crash*) Cilli!

(*Surprised and horrified,* Cilli *gives a yelp and falls on to the chaise-longue in a dead faint*)

Good gracious! The thrill must have been too much for her. (*He moves towards her*) Cilli! (*He slaps her wrists—to no effect*) Come back to me, little rose-bud. It's your Hansi-Pansi. (*He feels in his pockets*) Now where did I put that "Manual of First Aid—Troops, for the use of"? (*He finds it*) Ah! Here it is. (*He thumbs through it*) Acne . . . Eczema . . . Fainting Fits. (*He reads*) Fainting Fits: Open all windows. Burn a feather under the nose. (*He looks around*) Open all the windows —in a shop? Burn a feather? This isn't a chicken run! (*He reads again*) "In extreme cases all tight underwear should be loosened." Now *that* sounds more like what the doctor ordered. *All* tight underwear, eh? (*He prepares for the appropriate action*)

CILLI (*sitting up immediately and slapping his hand away*) That will be quite enough of *that!*

HANS (*anxiously*) You don't think that—er—just as a precaution . . . ?

CILLI (*seizing his face and looking at it incredulously*) Great Heavens, it's *you!*

HANS. You wouldn't care to faint again?

CILLI. *What* are you doing in that ridiculous uniform?

HANS (*elaborately casual*) As a matter of fact I joined the Army.

CILLI. You joined the Army? What regiment? The Seventeenth Underwear Looseners?

HANS (*hurt*) Cilli, *I* am in the Imperial Guard.

CILLI (*examining one of his buttons*) So you are! Whatever made you do such a thing?

HANS. *You* did!

CILLI. *Me?*

HANS. That's right. When I was just the delivery boy here you wouldn't even look at me.

CILLI. Now, Hansi, that isn't true . . .

HANS. No, you wouldn't. Like the rest of 'em you were too busy rolling your big eyes at the officers. (*He gives a quick, exaggerated impression of a lovesick girl*) So I said to myself: "Hansi, there's only one way out of it. *You* must be a soldier, too. *You* must be prepared to do or die—even if it kills you!"

CILLI. Oh, Hansi! You really loved me as much as *that?* My hero! (*She throws herself into his arms*)

HANS (*embracing her*) My golly, it *worked!*

CILLI (*looking up at him*) Hansi, I have the strangest feeling. It must be romance at last.

HANS. Either that or my cartridge belt is sticking into your corsets! (*He releases her and straightens his belt*)

CILLI. My brave boy, you must tell me everything. What's the Army like?

HANS. It's a real man's life, (*he shudders*) horrible!

CILLI. I can hardly believe that my Hansi joined up.

HANS. He can hardly believe it either. One day delivering roses . . . the next grooming the regimental goat. (*He holds his nose*) Whew!

CILLI (*fondly*) My Hansi a he-man at last. And he used to be such a drip!

HANS. Remember many a drip has worn away a heart of stone.

CILLI. Not *you.* If you'd been left alone with *Venus* you wouldn't have known what to do.

HANS. Well, you wouldn't have expected me to take advantage of a woman without any arms? (*Fondly*) Thank Heaven *you're* no Venus!

CILLI (*recoiling indignantly*) Charming! (*She moves away*)

HANS (*following her*) No, Cilli. *You're* a real live lady . . . with two of everything! (*He throws his arms round her*) My tiger-lily! My little wolf-woman! (*He plasters her with kisses*) I *adore* you.

CILLI (*breaking free*) H-h-hansi! (*Accusingly*) *Where* did you pick up that fancy technique?

HANS. Technique? (*Delightedly*) Have *I* got technique? Oh, goody, goody!

CILLI. All that "tiger-lily, wolf-woman" stuff. The most romantic thing you ever said to me in the old days was, "Well, how about it?" (*Accusingly again*) Hans, you've been *working* at it!

HANS (*proudly*) Well, a man can't be with Count Max without picking up a thing or two . . .

CILLI (*thrilled*) Count Max? Don't tell me you've been with *him* all this time?

HANS (*nodding proudly*) I'm his right-hand man, his personal assistant. What a man! What elegance, what charm; his wonderful way with the women! Just let *him* get a girl in a dark corner; he can read her like a book.

CILLI. How can he read *in the dark?*

HANS (*demonstrating with his fingers*) Braille!

CILLI. Oh, Hansi, I *am* proud of you.

HANS (*indicating the chaise-longue*) Come over here and I'll make you prouder still!

CILLI. Hansi, you're so fierce and masculine . . .

HANS. And *you're* so frail and feminine!

"IT'S SUCH A TRICKY THING, THIS LOVE" No. 4

CILLI. Hans, romance is very nice,
  That confetti lark and rice.
  But till I'm asked to sign
  Upon the dotted line,
  I'll still remember Momma's advice!

  It's such a tricky thing, this love,
  A rather sticky thing, this love,
  To ev'ry female He-Male Man's a king
  But never say "I will" until those church bells ring!
  Think what you're doing with this love
  And don't start cooing like a dove,
  Until you're lined up, signed up, floating down the aisle!
  It's such a tricky thing, this love!

HANS. Cilli, life's been like a song
Since the day you came along,
The joyous verve of you,
The luscious curve of you,
They make my heart-beat sound like a gong!

It's such a tricky thing, this love
A kiss-me-quickie thing, this love,
Oh, what a Cleopatra you must be
To make a Mark Antonio of little me!
There's nothing slow about this love
Away we'll go without a shove,
And you'll surrender, tender bird of my desire!
It's such a tricky thing, this love!

(*The number finishes with a comedy dance routine in which* CILLI *at first acts coy, while* HANS *pursues her wolfishly; then they exchange moods.*
As the music finishes, HANS *takes* CILLI *in an embrace so fierce that they both lose their balance, trip over the kit-bag, and cannon into the* L *end of the counter, bringing a tier of flower-pots down with a crash.* CILLI *scrambles hastily to her feet as she hears* GRETA *approaching.* HANS *stays on the floor, partly concealed by the chaise-longue.* GRETA *enters* R)

GRETA *'not seeing Hans*) Cilli, I told you to look after the shop— not break it up! What on earth happened?
CILLI. I'm sorry, Miss Greta, b-but it was—er——

(HANS *rises shakily to his feet*)

—(*indicating Hans*) *this* on earth!
GRETA (*not recognizing Hans*) So you've got a soldier at last? (*To Hans*) She always needed a military escort.
CILLI. Yes, but look *who* I've got!
GRETA (*after an astonished look*) Good gracious! It's Hans!
HANS (*saluting smartly*) Miss Greta!
CILLI. My Hansi, back from manœuvres. And, guess what? He's personal assistant to Count Max!
GRETA. Not really, Hans? But that's wonderful.

(MAX *enters up* L *and listens with amusement.* HANS, *busy picking up the spilled flower-pots, does not see him*)

CILLI. Wherever the Count goes my Hansi goes too. He's a big man in the regiment. The Count can't go anywhere without him!

(MAX *begins to laugh. The others turn in surprise.* HANS *registers guilt and then looks imploringly at Max*)

MAX (*coming down* C) You never said a truer word, Cilli. Look at these boots of mine. What a shine, and all his work! I've got the finest batman in the regiment! (*He slaps Hans on the shoulder, nearly sending him flying*)
CILLI (*sternly*) So *that's* all you are! (*She grabs hold of Hans*) Come

along—batman. I think we should have a nice little talk! (*She takes hold of his ear and propels him off* R)

HANS' EXIT   No. 4a

MAX (*amused, and turning to Greta*) And how about us? (*He takes her by the hand*) I wanted to see you alone.

(*The music begins*)

"MY PRETTY FLOWERS"   No. 5

GRETA (*speaking over the music; teasingly*) Was it so awfully important?

MAX (*seriously*) *I* think it was. You see, I love you more than anything in the world. I can't imagine life without you.

GRETA (*enchanted*) Oh, Max!

MAX (*with mock solemnity*) But then there's Paris . . .

GRETA (*scornfully*) Paris! (*She takes the telegram from her pocket and throws it into a waste basket, which is under the table*) So much for Paris! Oh, Max, this *must* be a dream.

MAX. Don't be afraid of waking. You won't find me gone.

GRETA (*momentarily sad*) I wonder. "The Count and the Flower Girl" . . . it's too like a fairy-tale.

MAX. "They lived happily ever after."

GRETA. That's what the story says. But supposing something were to take you away from me?

MAX. It happens—in a soldier's life. But you don't imagine I'd forget you?

GRETA (*with a shrug*) I'm talking a lot of wild nonsense. Let's just live for this wonderful evening . . . and let me give you something to remind you of *that!* (*She takes a red rosebud from a vase on the counter, kisses it, and puts it into his tunic. Then she begins to sing*)

> Sweet are the posies I fashion
> Sweet as the summer we've spent,
> Red with the roses of passion
> From the garden of heart's content.
> Only flowers can sweeten with their spell
> Lonely hours when we have said farewell!
> Roses will carry my memory of you,
> Every petal a dream come true.
>
> My pretty flowers will be
> A token when we part,
> Each coloured flower a word
> I've spoken in my heart.
> Though petals may fade by morning
> Just don't be afraid—
> Their warning be scorning.

> There'll be a fragrance
> You'll remember in the air,
> And you'll have roses in December
> While you care.
> Then one happy day—
> I'll take you in my arms and say:
> "My pretty flowers have kept you
> True to me".

MAX *and* GRETA (*singing together*)
> My pretty flowers will be
> A token when we part,
> Each coloured flower a word
> I've spoken in my heart.
>
> Though petals may fade ^{with the}/_{by} morning
>
> ^{Never}/_{Just don't} be afraid—
> Their warning be scorning.
> There'll be a fragrance
> You'll remember in the air,
> And you'll have roses in December
> While you care.
> Then one happy day—
> I'll take you in my arms and say:
> "My pretty flowers have kept you
> True to me".

(MAX *takes Greta in his arms and kisses her. They are interrupted by* HANS *who enters* R, *a shoebrush in his right hand and a woman's shoe over his left. He appears to be very agitated*)

MAX (*breaking away from Greta*) Why, Hans; what's the matter?
HANS. She's at it already, sir. Six pairs of her number nines . . . and make sure she can see her face in 'em.

(GRETA *laughs at him. At that moment* PRINCE SCHMETTOFF *enters up* R, *beyond the window. A tall, soldierly figure with grey hair, moustache and side-whiskers, he is dressed in Viennese hunting-style costume*)

MAX (*to Hans*) Well, after those stories of yours, I think you had it coming to you.
HANS (*spotting the Prince through the window*) And with due respect, sir, I think you have something coming to *you*.
MAX. What the devil do you mean?
HANS. From just up the street, sir. (*He points* R) A small but powerful force advancing in this direction . . . and I *think* it may be an offensive.

(*The* PRINCE *crosses from* R *to* L. *behind the window*)

GRETA. Whatever are you talking about, Hans?
HANS. It's the Count's father, Miss Greta. It's Prince Schmettoff!

GRETA. Oh, dear!

MAX. Damn it, what can he be after?

GRETA. Oh, Max, you don't think that he . . . ?

MAX (*pointing to the* R *exit*) In there, darling, and leave me to find out!

(GRETA *exits* R *with a worried glance backward*)

HANS. I'll look after Miss Greta, sir.

MAX. No, Hans, you'll stay right here . . . you're going to be my alibi!

(*As* HANS *stands blinking, the* PRINCE *enters up* L)

PRINCE (*at the head of the steps*) Well, Max . . . ?

MAX (*saluting*) Good evening, Father. If you'll forgive me just a moment? (*He rounds fiercely upon Hans*) So you admit that you've been pestering the delivery girl of this establishment with your attentions?

HANS. With my—er—what, sir?

(*The* PRINCE *puts in his monocle and watches the scene with bewilderment*)

MAX (*irritably*) Attentions!

HANS (*springing to attention*) Sir!

MAX. A pretty state of affairs.

HANS. I wouldn't go as far as "pretty", sir. I'd settle for "cuddly-looking".

MAX. Silence! Any complaint of your behaviour in the future I'll have you confined to barracks and out of harm's way.

HANS (*hanging his head in mock humility*) Yes, sir.

MAX. Now get out of here—and don't come back!

HANS. N-no, sir. (*Turns and marches out* R *with a heavy wink to Max*)

(MAX *has difficulty in keeping a straight face as he watches Hans go. Then he turns to his father*)

MAX. A little matter of—er—discipline. It's good to see you again, Father . . .

PRINCE (*quizzically*) Is it? I notice you didn't precisely hurry home to see me when you got back.

MAX. I'm sorry, sir, but there *is* a little thing called "duty".

PRINCE (*drily*) Mm! I'm delighted to learn that you take *something* seriously!

MAX (*with a shrug*) Come on, Father. What is it *this* time? My tailor? The wine merchant?

PRINCE. For once, Max, neither. While you were away I had an interview with the Emperor . . .

MAX. With the Emperor? Phew! I hope *you're* not in trouble, too?

PRINCE. Sit down, Max, this is serious . . .

MAX (*sitting on the chaise-longue*) Well?

PRINCE. His Majesty wanted to talk to me about *you!*

MAX. About me? Phew! (*Hopefully*) Promotion?

PRINCE. No.

MAX (*alarmed*) Not—er . . . ? (*He turns down his thumbs, registering demotion*)

PRINCE. Neither. The Emperor considers, as I do, that it's time you got married and settled down.

MAX (*startled*) Wha-at? (*He rises*)

PRINCE. You'll get your promotion all right—but first of all you'll have to show some sign of taking life seriously.

MAX. And did His Majesty suggest whom I was to honour with my "serious attentions"?

PRINCE. Yes, Max, he did.

MAX. And who is it to be?

PRINCE (*impressively*) His own cousin, Helga von Eberhardt!

MAX. The Countess Helga?

PRINCE (*nodding proudly*) It's a very great honour for our family!

MAX. But it's absurd! Helga and I hardly know each other. And we certainly don't love each other.

PRINCE. *Love?* My good boy, you weren't born into a world where young people marry because they're "in love". The betrothal is to be announced as soon as possible.

MAX. It's out of the question, Father. You see . . .

PRINCE (*cutting in, icily*) I see nothing, except that you have been making a fool of yourself with some cheap little shop girl!

MAX. You're not to speak of her like that!

PRINCE. And why not?

MAX. Because I happen to love her, that's why.

PRINCE. *Love?* Bah, nonsense! A casual affair that can be easily settled with a cheque. Make what excuses you can, Max, and come home at once! (*He turns and mounts the steps*) Believe me, my boy, it's the sensible thing to do!

(GRETA *enters* R, *hesitantly. The* PRINCE *stares coldly at her.* GRETA *curtsies, but the* PRINCE *ignores her and exits up* L)

GRETA. He's found out about us, Max—is that it?

MAX (*forcing a smile*) No, darling, nothing of the kind. Just the normal family squabble. Bills, bills and bills! I'm afraid I've been rather extravagant.

GRETA (*with relief*) Was *that* all? Well, that's something I'm going to cure you of!

MAX (*taking her hands, with adoration*) You really *are* too good to be true.

(*Off stage, in the distance, the* OFFICERS *and* GIRLS *are heard returning. As they arrive they sing a reprise of the* Marching Song of The Guard, *unaccompanied, which sounds rapidly nearer*)

GRETA. No more parties. You promise?

MAX (*solemnly*) No more parties. (*He laughs*) Except for the one that's on the way now!

(GRETA *and* MAX *turn gaily up stage to welcome* ERNST *and* JOHANN *who lead the return of the* OFFICERS *and* GIRLS. *They carry boxes of wine-glasses, and the others carry bottles.* HANS *and* CILLI *enter* R *and take the glasses and bottles, setting up an informal bar on the shop counter*)

VICKI. Why, look! If it isn't Hans!

(*All the* GIRLS *react*)

FRIEDL (*advancing on him with welcoming arms*) Hansi!
CILLI (*interposing sternly*) You leave my hero alone. (*She flourishes a corkscrew*) He's got work to do!

"WINE, WOMEN AND WAR"   No. 6

MAX, ERNST *and* JOHANN (*singing together*)
> Three things no man should miss
> Made for a man's delight.
> Give me girls who can kiss
> All through a summer night.

MAX.
> Seek your enjoyment where mine is
> Deep in a cellar where wine is.
> Add one single thing more—

MAX, ERNST *and* JOHANN (*together*)
> Soldiers were made for war!

MAX.
> Wine, women and war
> Are things we adore.

ERNST
> Fate we can defy
> With a glass of Tokay.

JOHANN.
> Dull moments we cheat
> With a kiss that's discreet.

MAX.
> Wine and women we desire,
> Till the guns begin to fire,
> Then war's the only thing
> Man can require to inspire.

MAX, ERNST *and* JOHANN (*together*)
> Then war's the only thing
> Man can desire.

MAX.
> Wine, woman and war
> To the coward are a bore.

ERNST.
> Though bottles may pass
> He's afraid of a glass.

JOHANN.
> Too scared to respond
> To the lips of a blonde.

MAX.
> If he's willing but he's weak,

> If he's too afraid to speak,
> He'd better leave it to those
> Whose technique is unique.

Max, Ernst *and* Johann (*together*)
> He'd better leave it to
> Those with technique.

(*All the* Officers *sing a refrain, and the* Girls *sing a descant to* "*Ah* . . .*"*)

Officers.
> Wine, women and war
> Are the things we adore.
> Fate we can defy
> With a glass of Tokay.
> Dull moments we cheat
> With a kiss that's discreet.

Officers *and* Girls (*together*)

> Wine and women $^{they}_{we}$ desire,
>
> Till the guns begin to fire,
> Then war's the only thing
> Man can require to inspire.
> Then war's the only thing
> Man can desire.

(*The number builds to give the effect of an informal party, with much drinking and dancing. The waltz finishes with* Hans, *now* "*rather the worse for wear*", *being whirled off* R *by* Cilli. *A second or two after they disappear there is a loud crash off stage* R. *Everyone laughs.*

At that moment an Orderly *enters. He is in uniform and carries a sealed envelope. He crosses to Max and salutes*)

Orderly. Herr Count; a message from headquarters. (*He hands the envelope to Max, salutes and exits the way he came*)

Max (*moving down stage, opening the envelope*) Now what's happened? (*He reads and looks serious*)

(*The chatter and laughter dies.* Greta *watches anxiously.* Ernst *and* Johann *join Max*)

Ernst. Bad news, Max?

Max (*signing to him to be quiet*) It's from the Colonel. There's been trouble today—at Sarajevo. The Archduke was there on a state visit. He's been assassinated . . . !

Johann. Whew!

Max. I'm to report to Headquarters at once.

Ernst. But, Max. You know what *this* could mean?

Max (*seeing Greta's anxious expression*) That's enough. (*He turns to Greta with a smile*) Well, darling . . . ?

Greta. Max, you're leaving me. I know you are.

(Everyone *is silent*)

MAX. Only to see the Colonel. The Old Man is a regular fuss-pot these days.

GRETA. Don't go, Max—please don't.

MAX (*tenderly, putting his hand under her chin*) You want to get me court-martialled for disobeying orders? (*He looks around*) Well, a cheerful collection we've become. Let's have a toast before I go. (*He takes a glass and raises it*) To Greta!

ALL (*raising glasses*) To Greta!

MAX. And to Vienna, the city of our birth. The finest city in the world. Vienna! God bless you!

ALL. Vienna!

"GOOD-NIGHT VIENNA"   No. 7

MAX. City of love and laughter,
Heaven of hearts that seek romance,
All through the nights of summer
Under the stars you dance.
Now is the hour we leave you,
Parting before the day begins.
Sleep till the sunshine wakes you,
Dream to the sweet violins.

Good-night, Vienna,
You city of a million melodies.
Our hearts are thrilling
To the strains that you play
From dawn till the daylight dies.
Good-night, Vienna,
Where moonlight fills the air with mysteries,
And eyes are shining to the gypsy guitars
That sing to the starry skies.
Enchanted city of Columbine and Pierrot,
We know the magic of your spell.
Of our romances you're the hero.
Now is the time to say "Farewell".
Good-night, Vienna,
Now lovers kiss beneath your linden trees.
The world is waiting on the edge of the day,
Just waiting to say "Good-night".

FULL COMPANY.
Good-night, Vienna,
You city of a million melodies.
Our hearts are thrilling
To the strains that you play
From dawn till the daylight dies.
Good-night, Vienna,
Where moonlight fills the air with mysteries,
And eyes are shining to the gypsy guitars

          That sing to the starry skies.
          Enchanted city of Columbine and Pierrot,
          We know the magic of your spell.
          Of our romances you're the hero.
          Now is the time to say "Farewell".
          Good-night, Vienna,
          Now lovers kiss beneath your linden trees.
          The world is waiting on the edge of the day,
          Just waiting to say "Good-night".

GRETA.   City of silver starshine,
          Folding your petals like a rose,
          Sad are the hearts that love you,
          Sad that the day must close.
          Lights on the Danube gleaming,
          Laughter that lingers on the breeze,
          Sweet be the dreams you're dreaming,
          City of hearts at ease.

(*The* OFFICERS *and* GIRLS *repeat the refrain, while* MAX, GRETA, VICKI *and* FRIEDL *sing a descant to* "*Ah . . .*")

OFFICERS *and* GIRLS.
          Good-night, Vienna,
          You city of a million melodies.
          Our hearts are thrilling
          To the strains that you play
          From dawn till the daylight dies.
          Good-night, Vienna,
          Where moonlight fills the air with mysteries,
          And eyes are shining to the gypsy guitars
          That sing to the starry skies.

(*Now* MAX *and* GRETA *take up the lyric, while the remainder of the* COMPANY *harmonize to* "*Ah . . .*")

MAX *and* GRETA.
          Enchanted city of Columbine and Pierrot,
          We know the magic of your spell.
          Of our romances you're the hero.
          Now is the time to say "Farewell".

FULL COMPANY.
          Good-night, Vienna,
          Now lovers kiss beneath your linden trees.
          The world is waiting on the edge of the day,
          Just waiting to say "Good-night".

(*As the applause dies at the end of the number,* ERNST *crosses to Max*)

ERNST. Now; what about the Colonel?

MAX (*crossing to Greta*) Darling, I *must* go. We'll meet, as we arranged, at the House in the Trees. (*He kisses her swiftly, hesitates as though he wanted to add something, then turns and exits quickly up* L)

(GRETA *makes a half-movement to follow him*)

VICKI. Don't look so worried, Greta. You'll see him again soon.
GRETA. Who says I'm worrying? I will, though, if you girls don't get tidied up and ready to leave.
JOHANN. We'll go and help them.
GRETA. Johann, I said "tidied"!

(*Laughing, the* GIRLS *run off* R *with the* OFFICERS)

MELOS   No. 7a

(*As* GRETA *looks round, seemingly a little "lost",* HELGA *enters up* R, *outside the window. She is a girl of aristocratic appearance, fashionably dressed. As she enters* GRETA *moves to meet her*)

GRETA. Good evening, Fräulein . . .
HELGA. I'm afraid I'm rather late.
GRETA. Not at all. What can I show you?
HELGA. I don't need anything immediately. I want to order for a month from today. (*She takes a slip of paper from her handbag*)
GRETA (*taking up an order-book*) Certainly, Fräulein. (*Writing*) For July the twenty-eighth . . .
HELGA (*reading from the slip of paper*) Twenty dozen red roses . . . and twenty dozen yellow roses . . .
GRETA (*to herself, writing*) . . . yellow roses.
HELGA. Twelve dozen carnations, red and white—the scented ones—they're for the table. And some of those big hydrangeas to decorate the ballroom.

(*A burst of teasing laughter comes from the* OFFICERS *and* GIRLS *off stage*)

(*Glancing to* R *with a smile*) That sounds like a party . . .
GRETA. It *will* be a party—a little later.
HELGA (*apologetically*) I know I'm keeping you . . .
GRETA. It's a pleasure, Fräulein. You mentioned hydrangeas . . .
HELGA. Yes, about a dozen, I think. If necessary we can always send for more. That will be all. To be sent to the Schmettoff Palace.

(*The Melos stops*)

GRETA (*dazedly, after a pause*) To—the—*Schmettoff* Palace?
HELGA (*casually*) Yes, they're for my betrothal party. To Count Max, you know.
GRETA. I see. And *your* name, Fräulein?
HELGA. The Countess Helga von Eberhardt. I must go now. I have a feeling I'm holding up your party.
GRETA (*almost inaudibly*) Not at all, Fräulein . . .
HELGA. Good evening . . . and many thanks. (*She exits the way she came*)

FINALE   No. 8

GRETA (*over the music, emotionally*) Twenty dozen red roses . . . twenty dozen yellow roses . . . to be sent to the . . . oh, Max!

(*She sings*)   Only flowesr can sweeten with their spell
               Lonely hours when we have said farewell . . .

(*She breaks down and exits* L, *sobbing bitterly. The music stops.
From off* R *comes the sound of the* OFFICERS *and* GIRLS *singing the
"Marching Song", very much in party mood. The* GIRLS *enter, led by*
VICKI *and* FRIEDL, *who are accompanied by* ERNST *and* JOHANN. *The
other* OFFICERS *follow. The* GIRLS *are now dressed for the street, with
hats, capes, feather boas, etc.*)

VICKI (*as she enters*) Greta! (*She looks round*) She isn't here!

FRIEDL. She won't be a moment.

ERNST (*picking up a bottle*) Anyway, there's still some wine left.
Let's have another toast. Now let me think . . .

JOHANN. You *think*, old fellow, and (*taking the bottle*) I'll *drink!*

VICKI. Why not to Vienna once again? That's the toast of the
evening.

ALL. Yes, to Vienna!

(*The music begins again and they all sing*)

          Good-night, Vienna,
          You city of a million melodies.
          Our hearts are thrilling
          To the strains that you play
          From dawn till the daylight dies . . .
          Good-night, Vienna,
          Where midnight fills the air with mysteries . . .

(*The* PRINCE *enters* L, *and the singing stops abruptly*)

PRINCE (*eyeing them coldly*) One moment! Is Fräulein Greta here?

(*A cymbal roll begins, under the scene*)

VICKI. Well—er—no, Your Excellency.

(GRETA *enters, through the crowd, followed by* CILLI)

GRETA. Yes, I am here. And what is it you want?

PRINCE. I understand, Fräulein, that my son has been carrying
on some kind of flirtation with you.

GRETA. We love each other, if that's what you mean.

PRINCE. We won't argue over the exact nature of the relationship
between you; that is no longer of any importance. At the special
request of the Emperor he is going to marry a lady from a rather
different world!

ALL (*with utter surprise*) Wha-at? (*They* ALL *exchange bewildered
glances*)

GRETA (*to the Prince*) How you must have enjoyed telling me that. But as a matter of fact I knew it already!

VICKI (*incredulously*) Greta . . . ?

PRINCE. Then that saves us a great deal of unpleasantness. You will not of course expect to see him again.

GRETA (*her voice trembling*) I shall not expect to see him again—ever! Now will you please go!

PRINCE. As you please. (*He bows, distantly*) Good night. (*He exits*)

VICKI (*after a long silence*) But, Greta! Tonight? The party?

GRETA (*smothering her feelings*) We're going to have our party, all of us.

FRIEDL (*dizzily*) We *are?*

GRETA (*loudly and on edge*) Yes, and it's going to be a *wonderful* party. It's going to be my farewell. (*She picks up the crumpled telegram*) Of course, Max and I were good friends and we've had fun together, but fun isn't everything. (*She uncrumples the telegram*) I've been invited to sing in Paris . . . and I'm going. Yes, and it's all going to be wonderful! So that's why we're having a party—at the House in the Trees, just as we arranged it. (*Her voice is trembling, but she just manages to hold up*) So come on, Ernst, Vicki, Johann, Friedl . . . *Come on.* My party! Paris! Oh, isn't it all fantastic?

(*The music picks up again*)

ALL (*singing*)

> The world is waiting on the edge of the day,
> Just to say "Good-night,
> Vienna, good-night!"

VICKI *tries to comfort* GRETA, *but she wrenches away, bravely takes Friedl's hat, puts it on her head with defiant humour and marches bravely out, followed by every eye, as—"*

the CURTAIN *falls*

ACT II

Scene—*The Garden of the Schmettoff Palace, the evening of 28th July 1914.*
At R, *slightly angled towards* C, *stands the entrance to the ballroom
reached by a flight of stone steps, a small terrace and a pair of handsome
glazed doors. Above this from* R *to* L *runs a high wall of weathered brick
hung with rambler roses. In the wall* L *of* C *there is a wrought-iron gateway leading to a path. On* L *stage are flower-beds, overarching trees and
ornamental hedges, between which are various exits to* L. *On stage,* L *of* C,
*stands a stone garden seat. Beyond the wall is a starry sky-cloth with cut-out
silhouettes of trees against it. The garden is in moonlight, but from the
ballroom streams light and the sound of voices.*

When the Curtain *rises, the stage is filled with* Guests, *the* Ladies *in
ball dresses, the older* Gentlemen *in white tie and tails, the younger
Gentlemen *in military uniform. On the terrace stands the* Prince *in
conversation with the* Baroness, *a grey-haired aristocrat. The* Prince
is in "tails" adorned with an impressive array of decorations. To R *and* L
of the ballroom entrance are uniformed Flunkeys.

"VIENNA WALTZ BALLET"　　　No. 9

Chorus. Vienna and the magic of romance
　　　　Vienna and the rhythm of the dance.
　　　　Ah-ah, Ah-ah,
　　　　For ever may we dance to this refrain,
　　　　And never may it end.
　　　　So hold me in this rhythm of delight,
　　　　Never let me go again.

(*The waltz continues*)

　　　　You and I under a velvet sky
　　　　Sway to the orchestra, thrilling with delight,
　　　　Caught in a melody magical and bright.
　　　　You and I, while there are stars on high,
　　　　Dancing and romancing as the night goes by.

(*The* Dancers *enter and perform the waltz ballet*)

　　　　Starlight in Vienna where the waltz is king
　　　　Prelude to a love-song happy hearts will sing.
　　　　Music so romantic at the end of day
　　　　Calls us like a rhapsody to magic lands far away.

(*The ballet continues*)

La-la, la-la-la, la-la
La-la, la-la-la.
Vienna and the magic of romance
Vienna and the rhythm of the dance.
Ah-ah, Ah-ah,
For ever may we dance to this refrain,
And never may it end.
So hold me in this rhythm of delight,
Never let me go again!

(*The number ends with a picture setting. As the applause dies, music begins again*)

EXIT MUSIC   No. 9a

(*The* DANCERS *exit, and the* GUESTS *begin to leave the stage. The* PRINCE *and* BARONESS *come down the steps to* C)

BARONESS. A delightful evening, Joseph.
PRINCE. My dear Baroness, I'm glad you find it so.
BARONESS. It's quite the event of the season. Dear Max and Helga! It seems a miracle that those two should have found each other.
PRINCE (*drily*) Yes, indeed. That is, if one believes in miracles these days.

(*They are now alone on the stage except for the* FLUNKEYS, *and a small group of* GUESTS *who remain on the terrace,* R)

BARONESS. Now, Joseph, don't tell me you're becoming cynical! Ah, *now* I understand. (*Roguishly*) A little match-making on the part of papa?
PRINCE. Well, perhaps you might call it that!

(JOHANN *enters through the garden gate, up* LC. *He is in dress uniform, wearing hat and sword. Seeing the Prince engaged, he hovers expectantly*)

BARONESS. Then I congratulate you. They make a perfect couple. Both so handsome, and so divinely happy.
PRINCE (*quizzically*) I—er—hope so. (*He sees Johann*) Ah, Lieutenant!

(JOHANN *salutes*)

(*Turning back to the Baroness*) If you will forgive me?
BARONESS. Of course. You must have many things on your mind tonight. Till later? (*She moves up the steps to the terrace,* R, *and joins the group of Guests*)
PRINCE (*to Johann*) Well, Lieutenant?
JOHANN. I carried out your orders, sir.
PRINCE (*impatiently*) Go on, man; what's happened?
JOHANN. No answer to the ultimatum yet. The War Ministry expects it before midnight.
PRINCE. Our friends the enemy are cutting it pretty fine.

JOHANN. A courier from Belgrade is due to arrive at any moment. (*Anxiously*) Your Highness doesn't think that . . . er . . . ?

PRINCE. That they'll fight? Pah! Not a chance. However, I'd rather you didn't say anything. We don't want the evening spoiled by a lot of nervous gossip.

JOHANN. Of course, sir! (*He salutes*)

(*The* PRINCE *walks up to the terrace where he is greeted by the* GUESTS. *The* PRINCE *and* GUESTS *exit, except for one* OFFICER *who remains on the terrace.* JOHANN *beckons to a* FLUNKEY *who comes down to him.* JOHANN *gives him his hat and sword and the* FLUNKEY *exits with them.* ERNST *and a pretty* DANCING PARTNER *enter from the ballroom. Seeing Johann,* ERNST *makes his apologies to the girl and gives her into the care of the* OFFICER. *The* OFFICER *and the* DANCING PARTNER *return to the ballroom as* ERNST *comes down to Johann,* C)

ERNST. Well . . . ?

JOHANN (*dejectedly*) Nothing doing. They're going to back out.

ERNST. Damnation!

JOHANN. Well, at least our evening won't be spoiled!

ERNST. For me it's been spoiled already. A fine crowd they are in there.

JOHANN (*sarcastically*) My dear feller, the very best families . . . what-what!

ERNST. And their frozen-faced daughters. The beauty I danced with just now asked me if I wouldn't mind putting my hand a little higher up her back!

JOHANN (*amused*) Poor Ernst! So much for your famous technique.

ERNST. I wish the devil we could get out of here.

JOHANN (*slyly, moving towards the gate up* LC) Or import some talent of our own?

ERNST. Nonsense, Johann. That would be out of the question.

JOHANN. You know the motto of the Imperial Guard? "The impossible we achieve immediately. Miracles take a little longer!" (*He opens the gate*) Welcome, ladies!

(ERNST *goggles as* VICKI *and* FRIEDL *enter. Both are in evening attire, well-made if a little "flashy"*)

VICKY *and* FRIEDL (*to Ernst*) Surprise! Surprise!

ERNST. But, Friedl, Vicki, those dresses?

JOHANN. I dropped the girls at the costumier on my way to the Ministry; picked them up again on the way back. (*Turning to Vicki and embracing her*) Darling.

ERNST (*embracing Friedl*) Angel! (*He looks anxiously at Johann*) Are you certain this is all right?

JOHANN. I'm not at all *certain*, but as long as we stay outside in the garden here . . .

VICKI. Stay *outside*? What's *inside*?

JOHANN. All sorts of things—including supper.

FRIEDL. You mean we don't get *anything to eat?*

JOHANN. We-ell, I think that *might* be arranged. (*He claps his hands commandingly*)

(HANS *enters from the side of the house, up* R. *He is in uniform, and carries a tray of sandwiches and glasses of champagne*)

HANS. Come and get it!
VICKI
FRIEDL }(*together*) *Hans!*
ERNST
FRIEDL. Johann, you think of everything!
ERNST (*a little jealous*) Well, *I* didn't get a chance.

(*They* ALL *gather round Hans*)

HANS. Who's for a nice meat tea?
FRIEDL. Goody-goody. (*She bites greedily into a sandwich, then makes a face*) Ew!
ERNST. What's the matter, darling?
FRIEDL. This jam tastes of fish!
JOHANN. So much for caviare!

(EVERYONE *laughs*)

VICKI (*after drinking*) Phew, doesn't champagne make your nose tickle!
JOHANN. And the things it can do to your *head!* (*He raises his glass*) Here's a toast to us. May we always be as happy as we are tonight.
HANS. It's in the firm's time, so I'll join you. (*He takes a glass and drinks*)
ALL (*clinking their glasses*) *Prosit!* (*They drink, and replace their glasses on the tray*)
ERNST (*to Friedl*) Your Highness, may I have the honour of this dance?

"DEAR LITTLE WALTZ"   No. 10

JOHANN (*bowing to Vicki, as the music begins*) Baroness? (*He turns to Ernst*) Careful of that wandering hand!

(HANS *exits up* R, *with the tray*)

VICKI, FRIEDL, ERNST *and* JOHANN (*singing together*)
            Dance with me
            To the strains of the mad violins.
            Columbines
            In the arms of their Harlequins.
            Magical music, you capture
            Hearts that are thrilling with rapture.
            Waltz with me
            Till the dawn of the new day begins.

(*As the number proceeds a few* OFFICERS *and* GIRLS *enter from the ballroom, R, seeking a breath of air before the supper interval, which is about to begin. They observe that the Quartette seem to be having a happier time than the more formal guests and gradually decide to join them. Bit by bit the stage fills as other* OFFICERS *and* GIRLS *enter from all parts of the garden)*

> Dear little waltz with the swinging tune,
> Dear little waltz that they played in June.
> Memories your music excites,
> You were our love song
> On those summer nights.
> Dear little waltz, 'neath your spell we've found
> Heaven made for two.
> To be caught in your arms
> Is just part of the charms
> Of that dear little waltz with you.

VICKI *and* FRIEDL.
> Swing with me
> To the lilt of the haunting strain.
> Two hearts
> Beating in time to the waltz refrain.
> Dance till the music has ended,
> Heaven to earth has descended.
> Life is short,
> I am here in your arms once again.

(EVERYBODY *waltzes*)

ALL.
> Dear little waltz with the swinging tune,
> Dear little waltz that they played in June.
> Memories your music excites,
> You were our love song
> On those summer nights.
> Dear little waltz, 'neath your spell we've found
> Heaven made for two.
> To be caught in your arms
> Is just part of the charms
> Of that dear little waltz with you.

(*The dance continues*)

> To be caught in your arms
> Is just part of the charms
> Of that dear little waltz with you.

(*As the number finishes* WILHELM, *Major Domo to the Prince, enters from the ballroom. He is a dignified, superior servant and wears a cut-away uniform of special design*)

WILHELM. Your Highnesses—Your Excellencies—Ladies and Gentlemen—supper is served!

(*The* GUESTS *begin to exit, some of the* LADIES *eyeing Vicki and Friedl with cold curiosity. Obviously, they are cattily discussing them sotto voce.* JOHANN, ERNST *and their* PARTNERS *reply to this chilly barrage with artificial smiles and gestures. With amorous eye plainly fixed upon Friedl (who is more than overplaying it) an* ELDERLY DIPLOMAT *lingers admiringly. His* PARTNER, *a lady of somewhat forbidding appearance, has reached the steps before she realizes that he is missing)*

PARTNER (*turning; tartly*) Ladislas!

DIPLOMAT (*turning, as though he had been stung*) Sorry, my dear. I was just admiring the er—view.

PARTNER. You were admiring the *what?* (*She studies Friedl through her lorgnette*) Come in to supper at once! (*She takes the Diplomat firmly by the arm, and hustles him into the ballroom*)

VICKI. Too bad! I thought he was rather a pet.

(WILHELM, *who has watched the previous scene with suspicion, comes down the steps*)

JOHANN. If you don't want to be thrown out, better confine your petting to me—(*seeing Wilhelm approaching*)—or see what you can do with *this* one. (*To Wilhelm*) Well, my good fellow, is there anything the matter?

WILHELM. I'm sorry, Lieutenant, but I must ask you for the names 'of these two ladies.

FRIEDL. Me? I'm Friedl . . .

ERNST (*cutting in hastily*) Friedl—er—Countess of Prague.

FRIEDL. Yes, and she's Vicki.

WILHELM. Vicki?

JOHANN. The Baroness Viktoria Tannebaum. I hope that satisfies you.

(*Unhurriedly,* WILHELM *takes a guest-list from his pocket and starts to check it*)

(*Ruefully*) I had an idea it wouldn't.

(MAX *enters from the ballroom,* R, *to the terrace. For the moment the others are too absorbed in Wilhelm's studied scanning of the list to notice him*)

MAX (*coming down the steps*) Well, what's the trouble here?

WILHELM. These two—er—female persons, Excellency. They do not appear to be on the list of guests.

MAX. Well, why the devil should they be? These ladies are here on business.

(WILHELM *raises his eyebrows*)

From the flower shop, man. It's their duty to attend to the decorations.

WILHELM. I'm sorry, Count Max. I had no idea. (*He turns to the girls*) Ladies, please forgive me. (*He exits in confusion*)

(*As soon as Wilhelm has left the stage, the* OTHERS *break into delighted laughter*)

VICKI } (*together*) { Sorry, Max, to have let you in for this.
FRIEDL }   { Please forgive us?

MAX. *Forgive* you? I have to *thank* you. (*Eagerly*) What news of Greta, Vicki?

VICKI. News of Greta? (*Sadly*) I'm sorry, Max, but we haven't any . . .

MAX. Not a word?

VICKI. No, Max, nothing. She left me a note asking me to look after the business and that was the last we heard of her.

FRIEDL. She must be in Paris by now.

MAX. In Paris? (*With a despairing gesture*) Oh, why the devil did I ever let her go?

FRIEDL. Why? Because you were a fool, *that's* why.

ERNST (*to Friedl*) Hey, there, steady on!

MAX. No, Ernst. Friedl is right. I *was* a fool, a weakling. A slave to the ridiculous system of a "marriage of convenience".

FRIEDL. Well, what can you do about it now?

MAX. I don't know. I only know that I'm going to do *something*. I can't go through with this mockery of a betrothal, it's out of the question . . . impossible.

VICKI (*gently touching his arm*) I believe you, Max. But I think you're in an awful jam.

(HANS *enters hastily from the ballroom*)

HANS (*signalling wildly*) Psst! Psst!
MAX. What is it, Hans?

(HANS *performs a ridiculous mimed impression of the Prince*)

My father?

HANS (*very proud that his mime has been identified*) Yes, sir. Rather good, wasn't it?

JOHANN (*taking hold of Vicki*) This is where we beat a retreat.

ERNST (*to Friedl*) Come on. This way, quick. (*He hustles her up stage*)

(JOHANN *and* VICKI *follow Ernst and Friedl up stage*)

VICKI (*looking back as she goes*) Au revoir, Max. (*Tenderly*) And good luck.

(ERNST *and* FRIEDL *exit through the gate, up* LC, *followed by* JOHANN *and* VICKI. *The moment they have gone, the* PRINCE *enters from the ball-room.* HANS *stands rigidly to attention, and the* PRINCE *glances angrily at him.* HANS *does an about-turn and exits up* R)

PRINCE (*coldly*) So there you are, Max.
MAX (*without enthusiasm*) Yes, Father. Here I am.
PRINCE. You realize that you are neglecting your guests?

MAX (*with a shrug*) *My* guests, sir?

PRINCE (*impatiently*) Well, then, yours and mine! They're here out of regard for both of us. What's wrong with you, Max? This should be one of the happiest evenings of your life.

MAX (*on edge*) Please! Do we have to go into that *again?*

(HELGA *enters from the ballroom. She is beautifully dressed, and wears a tiara*)

How often do I have to tell you that ... (*He breaks off as he sees Helga*)

PRINCE (*quickly following his gaze, and then going to Helga; smoothly*) Helga, my dear! Max and I were just talking about you.

HELGA (*a little quizzically*) Were you? Now that's very flattering.

PRINCE. He was coming to ask you for the next dance.

HELGA. Really?

MAX (*with obvious effort*) Of course. May I have that honour?

HELGA. Would you forgive me if I were to say "No"?

(*The* PRINCE *looks up, startled*)

I find it rather warm in there. I need a little fresh air.

PRINCE (*hastily*) Max shall escort you.

HELGA. No need to, Max. I'll join you later.

MAX. As you wish, Helga. (*He bows and exits to the ballroom*)

PRINCE (*smoothly apologetic*) The boy is a bundle of nerves tonight.

HELGA (*teasingly*) Is he the *only* one?

PRINCE (*with a little bow*) Touché! This is a very important occasion for all of us. (*He puts his hand in his pocket*) I would like you to see the betrothal ring, my dear. I have it here. (*He takes out a jewellery-box and opens it*)

HELGA (*genuinely impressed*) Oh, but it's beautiful. May I slip it on? Just for a moment.

PRINCE (*doubtfully*) That is unlucky, they say.

HELGA. Superstitions don't worry *me*, Your Highness. Not unless they turn out to be *true!* (*She takes the ring and slips it on her finger*) Let me wear it, just for a little while?

PRINCE (*still doubtfully*) Certainly, if you wish.

(HELGA *holds out her hand*)

(*He kisses her hand*) But not for too long. (*He exits to the ballroom*)

(HELGA *watches him go, then gives a sad little shrug. She looks at the ring on her finger as the music starts*)

"WHEN A WOMAN WEARS A RING"   No. 11

HELGA (*singing*)
> A girl is always waiting for the Spring
> To bring a man to suit her plan.
> A woman knows the day that life began—
> When on her hand love set a ring.

When a woman wears a ring
Upon her finger,
Telling of a lovely thing
To all the world,
Her news is broken
The sweetest way.
That golden token
Tells all there is to say.
When a woman wears a ring
Upon her finger,
Telling of a dream in Spring
To all the world,
Her eyes have spoken
The message from her heart,
For when a woman wears a ring
A song is in her heart.

A girl in love has news for all the world,
It cannot hold, it must be told.
The story of her heart is set in gold,
And from her hand, you'll understand.

When a woman wears a ring
Upon her finger,
Telling of a lovely thing
To all the world,
So sweet her story
As April rain
Turns fields to glory
When the sun breaks through again.
When a woman wears a ring
Upon her finger,
Telling of a dream in Spring
To all the world,
Her eyes are shining
As bright as stars above,
For when a woman wears a ring
No song can sing her love.

 (*During the applause,* HELGA *exits to the ballroom,* R. *At once,* HANS *enters, furtively, from up* R. *When he sees that the coast is clear, he skips excitedly across to* L)

HANS (*calling towards the garden*) Cilli! (*There is no reply*) Oh, Cilli, where *are* you? (*Still no reply*) Cilli!

 (CILLI *suddenly appears from behind a bush, very close to Hans*)

CILLI (*clapping her hand over Hans' mouth*) Sssh! Do you want me to get thrown out?
HANS (*struggling free*) But, Cilli, I have something to tell you.

Cilli. Then tell it to me back there. (*She tries to drag him off towards* L *stage*) No-one will see us down by the compost heap!

Hans (*on his dignity, resisting*) Down by the compost heap? What do you take me for, some cheap fertilizer? (*Disgustedly*) The compost heap! That's a fine place for romance!

Cilli (*scornfully*) For *romance?* Now, Hansi, haven't I told you a dozen times . . .

Hans (*cutting in*) I know. (*Giving an exaggerated imitation of her*) "No romance until we've got a place of our own."

Cilli. That's right! And what's been the result so far? All promises and no premises!

Hans. But everything's different now, Cilli. We *have* got a place. And it was all due to *you.*

Cilli (*puzzled*) Due to *me?*

Hans. Yes. You were the cause of my joining the Army.

Cilli (*with a shrug*) That's as may be.

Hans. No, that's as *was.* And my joining the Army was the cause of my Uncle Rudi forgiving me . . .

Cilli (*bored*) Anything more?

Hans (*proudly*) Yes. Uncle Rudi is so proud of me now that he's decided to leave us his premises in the Kaiserstrasse!

Cilli (*staring, open mouthed*) Oh, Hansi! Pinch me, I must be dreaming.

Hans. Certainly! (*He pinches her behind, forcefully*)

Cilli. Ouch! (*She slaps his hand away*)

Hans. Awake now? (*He threatens another pinch*)

Cilli (*backing hastily away*) Premises in the Kaiserstrasse? Why, it must be a *palace.*

Hans. We-ell, not exactly that.

Cilli. A villa, then?

Hans. Not even a villa. In fact it's a shop.

Cilli. A shop? You mean one of the big stores?

Hans. No, just one of the small ones.

Cilli (*ecstatically*) A small shop! I *love* the idea.

(Hans *blinks*)

What'll we be selling? Jewellery?

(Hans *shakes his head*)

Not—chocolates?

(Hans *shakes his head again*)

Leather goods?

(Hans *shakes his head*)

Let me think . . . the Kaiserstrasse . . . a dress shop? A hairdresser's? Not a *bank?*

(Hans *shakes his head vigorously*)

Thank God!

(HANS *goggles*)

Then—*what?*

HANS (*humbly*) It's, er, a Ham and Beef Shop.

CILLI (*slowly*) A Ham and Beef Shop?

HANS (*hastily*) With beigels and smoked salmon on the side!

CILLI (*bursting with ecstasy*) Oh, Hansi! A Ham and Beef Shop! A Ham and Beef Shop all of our own! (*She throws her arms around him and kisses him on the cheek*) That's for the beigels! (*She kisses the other cheek*) And that's for the smoked salmon! (*She breaks away from him*) I'm so happy. I'll marry you tomorrow!

HANS (*stunned by the denouement*) You mean that you actually *like* the idea?

CILLI. Like it? I'm crazy about it. It'll be so practical, Hansi. What we can't *sell* we'll be able to *eat!*

"A LITTLE DELICATESSEN FOR TWO"   No. 12

(*Throughout the following Musical Number*, HANS *and* CILLI *use illustrative comedy business*)

HANS.   In every sweet romantic play
          You'll run across that "small café"
          Where handsome lovers find
          Their happy ending.

CILLI.   Tho' full of wine and waltz refrains,
          No doubt it's rather short of drains
          The bathroom's down the garden—
          And needs mending!

HANS.   No "small café" for you and me,
          We'll find a better spot.
          Just listen while I tell you of
          The big idea I've got.

          When the wedding bells are over
          And our hearts are both in clover
          Then I'll tell you, darling, what we're going to do.
          Tho' our friends'll think us frantic,
          We'll be happy and romantic
          In a little delicatessen for two!

CILLI.   It will really be an idyll,
          Just like living in the middle
          Of a fairy-tale too perfect to be true.
          With the cheese and chipolatas,
          The anchovies and tomatoes
          Of our little delicatessen for two!

HANS.	I'll be serving the roll-mops.
CILLI.	I'll be cutting the ham.
HANS.	We'll be knee-deep in onions.
BOTH.	And we won't give a damn If there's room for a pram!

HANS.	When the atmosphere is balmy With the perfume of salami, And the gorgonzola starts to bill and coo!
BOTH.	Life'll be a bed of roses If we only hold our noses In our little delicatessen for two.

CILLI.	Behind the counter of our shop I'll work and work and never stop, And, oh, the lovely things I'll be preparing.

HANS.	I'll work like mad to earn my pay. I'll get up at the break of day And take the Bismark herrings For an airing!

CILLI.	Tho' Romeo and Juliet Found love among the flowers, I doubt if that romance of theirs Was tastier than ours!
	When I'm slicing up the salad Life will be a lyric ballad, Tho' the camembert smells rather like the zoo! I'll be whistling while I'm working. I'll adore each darling gherkin In our little delicatessen for two!

HANS.	We'll be living, willy-nilly, In a world of piccalilli. I'll be singing like a skylark in the blue. Yes, you'll get "The Men of Harlech" With a flavouring of garlic In our little delicatessen for two!

CILLI.	There'll be plenty of bus'ness.
HANS.	We'll have clients galore.
CILLI.	We've no need for assistants—
BOTH.	When the kids get to four They can work in the store.

CILLI.   And romance in such a setting
           We'll be surely not forgetting,
           When the long and busy day at last is through.
BOTH.   There'll be time to do our wooing
           While the sauercraut is stewing
           In our little delicatessen for two!

(THEY *dance*)

CILLI.   When I send you on manœuvres,
HANS.   Chock-a-block with horses' doovers,
BOTH.   In our little delicatessen for two!
           In our little delicatessen for two!

(HANS *and* CILLI *exit* R)

MELOS   No. 13

(*A shadowy figure can be seen through the gateway, up* LC. *It is* GRETA. *She slowly opens the gate and lets herself into the garden. She is wearing a broad-brimmed leghorn hat and carrying a light coat, as though she were in travelling costume. Looking pale and strung up, she stands for a moment, taking in the lighted ballroom, before stealing a little towards* C. *As she does so* MAX *and the* BARONESS *appear in the window, in conversation.* MAX *bows to the Baroness, and moodily starts to descend the steps.* GRETA *stiffens and appears unable to move away. It seems they must meet, when the* PRINCE *appears on the terrace*)

PRINCE. Max!

(MAX *swings round to face him*)

It's almost midnight, my boy. Time for the announcement. Our friends are waiting.
    MAX (*after a tense pause*) Very well, Father. (*Almost savagely*) They shall *have* their announcement! (*He walks stiffly past the Prince and into the ballroom*)

(*The* PRINCE *shrugs, and follows him*)

GRETA (*her voice breaking*) Oh, Max . . . Max! (*She turns to escape*)

(*A distant clock chime begins in the orchestra. An outburst of anticipatory chatter is heard from the ballroom.* JOHANN, VICKI, ERNST *and* FRIEDL *enter through the gate*)

ERNST. Twelve o'clock and poor old Max must be lining up for the start. (*He sees Greta*) *Greta!* Great Heavens, what are *you* doing here?
    VICKI
    JOHANN } (*together*) Greta!
    FRIEDL

GRETA. I just *had* to come, don't you understand? I *couldn't* leave Vienna till after tonight!

FRIEDL. You waited for *this?* Darling, you must be crazy.

VICKI (*intervening gently*) Friedl, that's unkind. When something really terrible has happened to you . . . you still hope and pray that it may turn out to have been only a bad dream.

GRETA (*emotionally*) Oh, Vicki! (*She buries her head in Vicki's shoulder*)

(*A fanfare sounds in the orchestra*)

WILHELM (*off* R) Your Excellencies, ladies and gentlemen, pray silence for His Highness the Prince Josef Schmettoff!

GRETA. I can't. Let me go!

VICKI (*restraining her*) Too late. You *have* to find out now.

(GUESTS *enter from all entrances*)

JOHANN (*to Vicki*) Look after her, we'll join you later. (*He beckons Ernst to follow him up stage*)

(VICKI *and* FRIEDL *lead* GRETA *down* L *where they can stand unobserved. The* GUESTS *are now crowding on stage, all eyes turned towards the french window from the ballroom. The* PRINCE, *with* HELGA *and* MAX *on either side of him, appears in the window. The* GUESTS *fall silent*)

PRINCE. Dear friends, it is now my proud and happy duty to announce formally the purpose of our celebration tonight—the betrothal of my son, Max, to Helga Maria, the beloved daughter of the late Archduke Karl August.

(*There is a slight rustle and murmur of appreciation from the* GUESTS. GRETA *registers pained emotion throughout the following scene*)

Therefore, according to tradition, I call upon you, Helga, to say whether you do freely betroth yourself to my son?

HELGA. I do . . . (*she pauses*) if that be also *his* wish!

PRINCE (*a little disturbed by her reply*) Well, Max . . . ?

(*Hands clenched,* MAX *stares straight ahead of him. There is a disturbed rustle among the* GUESTS)

(*Impatiently*) Max? We could not hear your reply.

MAX. I am sorry, Helga, that you should have been brought here —for *nothing*. I cannot honestly go through with this. I am in love with someone else!

PRINCE (*breaking a shocked silence*) What the devil . . . ?

MAX (*to Helga*) Can you ever forgive me?

PRINCE (*outraged*) Forgive you? For this scandalous insult? (*To Helga*) The boy must be out of his mind. My dear child, what can I say?

Helga. Say *nothing*. Leave this to *me*. I would like to speak to Max alone. (*She moves down stage*)

(*The* Guests *divide to let her past, then begin to exit* l *and* r)

Prince. Max, you will come with me . . . !

(*The music breaks off*)

Max (*shaking his head*) I'm sorry, Father. You heard what the Countess said. (*He breaks away and joins Helga*)

(*As the music flares up again the* Prince *stares after Max incredulously. Then he turns on his heel and strides into the ballroom.* Johann *signs to the girls, and* Vicki *and* Friedl *exit, while* Greta *remains transfixed.* Max *and* Helga *face each other without a word, as the orchestra plays Helga's theme. After a pause, she holds out her hand to him*)

(*He takes her hand and kisses it*) How can I explain?
Helga (*gently*) No need to, Max. The "explanation" is here, (*She indicates Greta*) in person.
Max (*incredulously*) Greta? (*He steps towards her*) Greta . . . ?
Greta (*retreating*) Max, let me go. I should never have come here. (*To Helga, imploringly*) Countess, tell him to let me go?
Helga (*almost sadly*) I have no right to do that.
Max. You knew about Greta all along?
Helga. Only since that evening when I went to order the flowers for—for another evening.

(Max *glances at Greta*)

No, Max, you mustn't blame her, she made a very brave pretence.
Max (*remorsefully*) Helga, what have I done to you?
Helga. Nothing—except to make me proud of you.
Max. Proud?
Helga (*with a nod*) That was an honest thing you did just now. But don't underrate the cost of it. Your father has taken it very badly and as for the crowd of conventional gossips (*she gestures towards the ballroom*) in there . . . ! (*She shrugs and turns to Greta*) Good-bye, my dear, look after him. Good-bye, Max. (*Softly*) I could have loved you but I know when I have lost the game. (*She turns and, without looking round, walks proudly into the ballroom*)
Greta (*with awe and respect*) She is a great lady.
Max (*nodding*) Very great—God bless her!

(*The Melos leads directly to the Introduction to No. 14*)

"JUST HEAVEN"   No.14

(*He speaks over the music*) My darling!
Greta. I can't believe it, Max.

Max. Neither can I.

(*He sings*)   Magical and strange
                   How the world can change
                   When a story finds
                   A happy ending.

Greta.   Luckless and alone,
              How could I have known
              Of this wonderland
              Where fairy-tales come true?

Max.   Just heaven,
              The world around us seems
              Just heaven—
              The landscape of our dreams.

Greta.   Never knew a moment so sweet.
              Drifting on a cloud
              With the stars at my feet.

Max.   Just heaven
              To see an angel smile
              So tender and true.

Both.   Winter's on the wing,
              We'll have everlasting Spring
              In this heaven of our world
              Beyond the blue.

Max.   Are we really free at last
              From the prison of the past?

Greta.   Free and bent for
              All our love was meant for.

              Days of gladness,
              Sweet midsummer madness,
              Words true and tender,
              Sighs of surrender!
              Darling, do not wonder,
              Darling, we are under
              The spell of this wonderful night.

MAX.   Dear, I adore you.
              I'm for ever for you.
              Though they had shamed you
              So proudly I proclaimed you.
              Not some foolish flower girl,
              No "for-just-an-hour" girl
              Who filled me with love and delight.

BOTH.   My pretty flowers will be
              A token when we part,
              Each coloured flower a word
              I've spoken in my heart.
              Though petals may fade with the/by morning
              Never/Just don't be afraid—
              Their warning be scorning.
              There'll be a fragrance
              You'll remember in the air,
              And you'll have roses in December
              While you care.
              Then one happy day—
              I'll take you in my arms and say:
              "My pretty flowers have kept you
              True to me."

MAX (*breaking away, and speaking over the music; tenderly*) I must
leave you now. I have to settle this business with my father.
GRETA (*doubtfully*) Max, I'm frightened. You don't think that
he'll . . . ?
MAX (*cutting in*) I can't think of anything but *you*. (*He takes her
hand*) Wait for me at the House in the Trees. I'll be with you as soon
as I can. (*He raises her chin*) My darling this is the last au revoir.
GRETA (*ecstatically*) Oh, Max!

      (*They kiss*)

(*She sings*)   Just heaven
                You gave me with a smile
                So tender and true.

BOTH.   Winter's on the wing,
                We'll have everlasting Spring
                In this heaven of our world
                Beyond the blue.

      (GRETA *exits, with a last backward glance at Max. As* MAX *is watch-
ing her go,* JOHANN *and* ERNST *enter excitedly from the ballroom. Excited
chatter can be heard off* R)

JOHANN. Max!
MAX (*with a shrug*) I know . . . I've ruined the party.
ERNST. Damn the party. That's all forgotten now!
MAX (*bewildered*) Forgotten? What do you mean?
JOHANN. The news has just come through, Max. *It's War!*

MELOS: DECLARATION OF WAR   No. 15

MAX (*speaking over the music, as though stunned*) War? You mean
they didn't give way?
JOHANN (*a happy soldier*) No. Orders have just come through. We
leave for the frontier at once.

(*The* PRINCE *enters from the ballroom*)

PRINCE. Max!
MAX (*interrupting*) Father, I'm sorry, but . . . !
PRINCE. We can forget that now. You've heard the news? Oh,
this is a proud moment for all of us!
MAX. But, Father, I can't go now . . .
PRINCE. But that's nonsense, boy. Your orders have come. You're
to entrain at once.
MAX. Let the rest of them go.
PRINCE. The rest of them, Max? What are you talking about?
MAX. I'm not leaving tonight. I made a promise to someone. It's
my duty.
PRINCE. Duty? *Your* duty is to your Country. You're a soldier.
This is war!
MAX. Did I ask to become a soldier? No! I'm a free man. I'm in
love . . . and you can all go to the devil.

(*There is a "distant" trumpet call from the orchestra, followed by the
sound of* MEN *singing the* "Marching Song of the Guard" *off stage,
unaccompanied. The voices swell up and die away as they pass. The*
PRINCE, JOHANN *and* ERNST *stand rigid, their eyes on Max.* MAX *begins
to falter*)

PRINCE (*as the voices begin to die*) Max . . . those are *your* men.
MAX (*to Johann, suddenly a soldier again*) Lieutenant!
JOHANN (*coming to attention*) Sir?
MAX. All officers are to report to barracks immediately.

(*The* PRINCE *registers obvious relief*)

JOHANN (*with enthusiasm*) Yes, sir! (*He beckons to Ernst and exits to
the ballroom*)

(ERNST *follows Johann off*)

MAX (*turning to the Prince; a little gingerly*) Well, Father, my
congratulations. So you have won after all.

PRINCE. No, Max. The victory wasn't mine. No matter what you may have felt for a moment, you would have gone.

(HANS *enters* R, *in the full equipment he had in Act I. Behind him,* CILLI *enters, loitering timidly*)

(*Seeing Hans and addressing him*) You there . . . !
HANS (*halting*) Me, sir?
PRINCE. See that the Count's kit is loaded—and be sharp about it.
HANS (*with an enormous salute*) Sir!
PRINCE. Come, my boy. There are good-byes to be said.

(*The* PRINCE *and* MAX *exit.* HANS, *importantly, holds his salute long after they have gone*)

CILLI (*in a commanding voice*) Hansi!
HANS (*turning smartly towards her*) Sir! (*He relaxes*) Oh, no, not *you?*
CILLI (*crossing to him impatiently, and pushing him off balance*) You heard what the gentleman said. Look sharp!

(HANS *stares at her*)

Well, what are you hanging about for? Get that kit loaded!
HANS. Now look here, Cilli . . .
CILLI (*cutting in*) Hurry up! You'll be late for the war.
HANS. Will I? That's *wonderful.*
CILLI. You've had your orders. Get cracking!
HANS. *Get* cracking? I'm cracking already. Cilli, you've no idea what it'll be like at the Front. (*He gives a series of violent war impressions, at the end of which he is on his knees*) Whe-e-e-ee! Bang! Pah-pah-pah!
CILLI. Is that the Front?
HANS. Yes.
CILLI. In that case you'd better go to the Back.
HANS. How can I, Cilli? I've got to be a Hero.
CILLI. Why do you have to do that?
HANS. Because of Uncle Rudi. If I'm not a hero, he'll take back the shop.
CILLI. Oh, well, that's different. Better make it the Front after all. Off you go.
HANS. Aren't you going to kiss me good-bye?
CILLI. Good-bye, Hansi. (*She gives him a quick peck*)
HANS. Is that the best you can do? Can't I have the full Soldier's Farewell? The warm embrace? The lingering plonker? A few tiny tears?
CILLI. But that would be soppy. Soldiers' sweethearts just don't do it.
HANS. Have it the way you like it, then. Bye-bye, Cilli. Look after the business. And send me a postcard! (*He slaps her on the behind and marches off through the gate up* LC)

(*The* OFFICERS *and* LADIES *enter from the ballroom, among them* JOHANN, ERNST, VICKI *and* FRIEDL. *All the* OFFICERS *are now wearing hats and swords.* CILLI *finds herself surrounded by emotional scenes of farewell*)

CILLI. Vicki! Friedl!

(*But the* GIRLS *are too busy with their tearful farewells to take any notice of Cilli. A trumpet call sounds. The* OFFICERS *break away and move to the gate, up* LC)

(*Emotionally*) Hansi. Oh, Hansi, darling, wait for me! (*She pushes her way past the others and exits through the gate*)

(*The* OFFICERS *follow through the gate as the* GIRLS *wave their last farewells. Among the last Officers to leave is* JOHANN. *When they have gone the* GIRLS *sadly turn away and exit* L *and* R. *As the stage clears* MAX *and the* PRINCE *enter from the ballroom*)

MAX. Good-bye, Father.
PRINCE. Good-bye, my boy. (*Gently*) I'm sorry there's been this trouble between us. But that's all over now.
MAX. It's generous of you to admit it. There's just one more thing you can do for me.
PRINCE. Anything you ask, Max.
MAX (*taking an envelope from his pocket*) Greta is waiting for me, at the Houses in the Trees. Have this letter delivered to her personally. It explains why I'm having to go away without seeing her. I'll get leave as soon as possible, and be with her again.
PRINCE (*taking the envelope*) Very well, my boy. (*He embraces Max*) And . . . good luck!

(JOHANN *returns hurriedly to the gateway, up* LC)

JOHANN (*impatiently*) Max!
MAX. Right away. (*He goes up to the gate, then turns*) There's only one thing I'm worried about; am I wise to leave Greta alone with you and that damned Schmettoff charm of yours! (*He grins, waves to the Prince, and exits after Johann*)

MELOS: FINALE No. 16

(*The* PRINCE *shrugs, and shakes his head doubtfully.* WILHELM *enters from the ballroom carrying a silver tray on which is a decorative cigar-box, a cigar-cutter and an old-fashioned flint lighter*)

WILHELM (*offering the tray*) A cigar, your Highness?
PRINCE. Thank you, Wilhelm.

The PRINCE *takes a cigar, cuts it fastidiously and puts it between his lips.* WILHELM *strikes the lighter and offers the flame. After an instant's hesitation, the* PRINCE *sets light to Max's envelope, and lights his cigar from it. Then he watches the envelope until it is burning well, finally dropping it to the ground and extinguishing the smouldering paper with his foot.*

The CURTAIN *falls*

ACT III

Scene—*The House in the Trees, on an evening after the War.*
*Formerly a well-known and popular rendezvous in the Vienna Woods,
the House in the Trees is a restaurant decorated in a somewhat theatrical
Tyrolean style. Up stage is a terrace with a flight of steps c leading down
into the restaurant. Through the terrace archways can be seen the blue night
sky and a glimpse of many tree-tops. Down L is a cocktail bar. Down R
double swing doors lead to the kitchen quarters. Centre is a small dance floor
around which are arranged a number of tables laid for supper. On both
the bar L and on a tall service-trolley, below the kitchen doors R, stands a
telephone. The R telephone has a long lead.*

When the Curtain *rises,* Waiters *and* Waitresses *in Tyrolean-style
costumes are arranging tables under the watchful eye of* Johann (*now
maître d'hôtel*) *and* Ernst (*who is now the wine waiter*). *There are no
customers, and the dance floor is empty.*

"COME TO THE HOUSE IN THE TREES" No. 17

Chorus. Come to the House in the Trees.
You'll find us anxious to please;
We know your wishes,
Our dishes are rare;
None can compare
With Cupid's bill of fare.
Love à la carte, if you please,
Served in the style Viennese.
That is the reason
We've kisses in season—
We can always find patrons for these,
At our dear little House in the Trees.

(*A telephone bell rings twice, in time with the music. The* Waiters *and*
Waitresses *all stare in surprise.* Ernst *grabs at the telephone on the
trolley R, and comes c with the receiver to his ear*)

Ernst. Ja! Who's speaking?
Ah—Herr Gru!
A table for two?

Chorus (*with relieved surprise*)
A table for two!

Ernst. Some quiet corner?
Incognito?
Ah—just so.

CHORUS (*significantly*)
    We know!

ERNST.   When shall we expect you?
    Ja! At eight?
    Orchids on plate?

CHORUS (*significantly*)
    All tête-à-tête.

ERNST.   All right, Herr Gru!
    Good-bye, thank *you!*

(*He puts down the receiver and* JOHANN *makes an entry in an order-book lying on the bar*)

CHORUS.   Book another table for two!

(*The picture on stage changes. The telephone rings again, in time with the music.* JOHANN *picks up the receiver from the bar* L *and listens*)

JOHANN.   Oh! *Frau Gru!*
    What can I do for you?
    You ask me has your husband
    Booked a table for two?

(*He puts his hand over the receiver and stares round in dismay*)

CHORUS.   Tell her he's not been here,
    Or she'll make a scene here.
    Keep the party clean here,
    Do!
JOHANN.   No, Frau Gru!
    Your husband's not been through.
    No doubt he's coming home
    To spend the evening with you.

(*He puts back the receiver, with a look of horror on his face*)

    Ah! Mein Gott!
    Whatever shall we do?
    His wife has booked a table, too!

CHORUS.   Come to the House in the Trees.
    You'll find us anxious to please;
    We know your wishes,
    Our dishes are rare;
    None can compare
    With Cupid's bill of fare.
    Love à la carte, if you please,
    Served in the style Viennese.
    That is the reason

We've kisses in season—
We can always find patrons for these
At our dear little House in the Trees.

(*During the last few bars of the number the* WAITERS *and* WAITRESSES *dance off. Only* ERNST *and* JOHANN *remain*)

ERNST (*the ever-cheerful*) Well, two tables booked already. That makes a start anyway.

JOHANN. You call it a start? I'd call it the finish! Our only two regular customers—and they have to come on the same evening? Old Gru, with that blonde popsy of his——

ERNST. Champagne—in magnums!

JOHANN. —and his mountainous missus with her gigolo, the prize-fighter!

ERNST. A Jeraboam of burgundy—and acres of steak!

JOHANN. And what happens when they meet each other here?

ERNST (*optimistically*) We-ell, perhaps we can charge 'em for the breakages. Two tables, four chairs, a couple of windows . . . (*He meets Johann's unresponsive glance*) Sorry, I can't keep it up. (*He crosses to Johann*) What's wrong with this place, Johann?

JOHANN. Nothing, except the fact that it's a failure.

ERNST. When Cilli first had the idea it sounded great. Reopen the famous House in the Trees!

JOHANN. Staff it with ex-officers, and a few titles thrown in!

ERNST. Bring back the atmosphere of the good old days!

JOHANN. That was our mistake, you can't being back the old days. The world's a different place. We should never lave let Hans and Cilli sell the delicatessen.

ERNST. We needed a job.

JOHANN. True enough. And now it looks as though we'll soon be needing one *again!*

(HANS, *who is now the bar-tender, enters. He is gaily humming the melody of* "The House in the Trees". ERNST *and* JOHANN *turn and stare at him in amazement*)

ERNST. Hans, are you all right?

HANS. Yes, I'm feeling fine. (*He continues humming as he crosses to the bar*)

ERNST. But you're *singing!*

HANS. Thank you for the compliment.

JOHANN. What have *you* got to sing about?

HANS (*with a puzzled look*) Now, Mr Johann, that's a very good question. What *have* I got to sing about? (*With a shrug*) I must have caught it from the missus.

ERNST. You mean Cilli's singing, too?

HANS (*nodding*) Uh-huh. She's upstairs yodelling in the bath.

JOHANN. Yodelling?

HANS. That's right. And playing with her rubber U-boat! When I asked her if she was feeling all right she told me to shut up, get downstairs, pour myself a drink, cross my thumbs—and pray! (*He pours three large brandies*) I suggest we make a threesome of it?

JOHANN. Anything, on a night like this.

HANS (*in military style*) Attention! Cross-thumbs! Down the hatch! Pray!

(*After following out the routine* HANS, ERNST *and* JOHANN *are left staring into space. Suddenly, the telephone on the bar rings, sharply and shrilly*)

(*Jumping, startled*) Ouch! I'd forgotten the thing worked!

(ERNST *steadies Hans as* JOHANN *grabs eagerly at the receiver.* FRIEDL *—now the cigarette girl, and* VICKI*—the cloakroom attendant, enter up* C)

JOHANN (*speaking into the telephone*) House in the Trees. A table for six?

(VICKI *and* FRIEDL *stop dead in their tracks in surprise, and stare incredulously*)

Certainly, madame. (*He rings off*)

(*The telephone* R *rings*)

HANS. Good gracious! They must be *infectious*, too!

ERNST (*hurrying to answer the telephone* R, *and speaking into it*) House in the Trees here. Have we room for *how* many? A party of eighteen? Of course, m'sieu.

(*The* WAITERS *and* WAITRESSES *begin to enter, chattering excitedly*)

(*He rings off and turns round to Johann*) Eighteen! Did you hear that?

JOHANN (*excitedly*) I most certainly did. (*He enters the order in his book*)

VICKI ⎱
FRIEDL ⎰ (*together; ominously*) So did *we!*

VICKI (*to Johann*) What is this? A big joke?

FRIEDL (*to Ernst*) Very funny! Ha-ha!

(*Both telephones ring simultaneously.* VICKI *dashes to answer the phone* L, FRIEDL *runs to the phone* R. *As they take the messages,* CILLI *enters up* C, *unnoticed by the others on stage. She is very smartly dressed, and is studying a newspaper*)

VICKI (*into the telephone*) Yes, the House in the Trees. Four tables for four? Yes, my man, we'll see what we can do. (*She replaces the receiver*) The head porter at the Hotel Kaiserhof!

FRIEDL (*into the telephone*) I can't promise, anything, Your Excellency, but we'll do our best to fit you in. (*She replaces the receiver*) The French Ambassador!

CILLI (*coming down* c) Well, are we sold out yet?
ALL (*turning to her*) Cilli!
JOHANN. Cilli, what have you been up to?
CILLI. Nothing much. I just thought I'd put a little advertise-ment in the evening paper. (*She hands the paper to Johann*) Page one. Rather good, I thought.

(*They* ALL *gather round Johann*)

JOHANN (*reading*) "Come to the House in the Trees. Unexpected New Year's Gala, presenting for the first time in Vienna, the inter-nationally famous singer Nina Musique!"

(EVERYONE *gasps incredulously*)

CILLI (*proudly*) Well, how about *that?*
ERNST. Nina Musique? You've booked Nina Musique?
CILLI (*nodding*) That's right.
JOHANN. The girl whose records run into millions?
CILLI. That's the one!
VICKI. And what does her *salary* run into? That is, if she really has agreed to make her début in a place like this?
FRIEDL. Oh, but she *has*. It says so in the papers.
VICKI (*pityingly*) Friedl, don't be so naïve!
FRIEDL. And you, Vicki, don't you be so bossy. We're not in the flower shop now. Remember, I'm the cigarette girl here—you're only cloaks.
VICKI (*eyes blazing*) Why, you stuck up little madam!
CILLI (*intervening*) Girls! Girls! Hans, bring me a glass of cham-pagne!

(HANS, *shaking his head in puzzlement, goes to the bar*)

Vicki, the rest of you, you've just got to believe in me. It was my dream for all of you to see this place full to the doors and tonight that's going to happen!

(HANS *brings a champagne bottle and fills a glass for her*)

This is going to be a really *happy* New Year . . . and I'm going to have the time of my life. (*She drinks down the champagne*)

(ALL *respond with enthusiasm*)

"YOU CAN TAKE ME OUT TO SUPPER　No. 18

(*She sings*)　　　Young men, old men,
　　　　　　　　　Shy men, bold men,
　　　　　　　　　Yankee millionaires,
　　　　　　　　　Men who deal in shares
　　　　　　　　　Lure me to their lairs.

FRIEDL.   Short men, tall men,
           Some men, all men,
           Singly or in pairs,
           When they're dying for me
           Bore me so!

CILLI.   But I've learned a lesson or two.
           When love wasn't true
           I bid it adieu!

VICKI.   Love, they say, can make
           The world go round.

CILLI   Well, so can champagne,
           I've found.

           You can take me out to supper
           In the most expensive style.

FRIEDL.   If you think that you can
           Win me that way
           Then it really won't be
           Worth your while.

VICKI.   Every thought of love I scupper,
           And I just resist its thrill.
CILLI, FRIEDL *and* VICKI.
           If you play a game of love
           It's the woman always pays;
           But at supper, man
           Must settle up the bill!

           Will there be caviare?
HANS, ERNST *and* JOHANN.
           Yes! Yes!
CILLI, FRIEDL *and* VICKI.
           Hurrah!
           Have you a motor car?
HANS, ERNST *and* JOHANN.
           Yes! Yes! A car!
CILLI, FRIEDL *and* VICKI.
           I love a car.
           Will there be oysters?
HANS, ERNST *and* JOHANN.
           Yes!
CILLI, FRIEDL *and* VICKI.
           I really must confess
           You are the most attractive lovers
           We have met so far.

           Will there be nectarines?

HANS, ERNST *and* JOHANN.
        Yes! Yes!
CILLI, FRIEDL *and* VICKI.
        What means!
        And powerful limousines?
HANS, ERNST *and* JOHANN.
        Yes! Fit for queens.
CILLI, FRIEDL *and* VICKI.
        Just give me coats of sable,
HANS.   Let me run a racing stable,
CILLI, FRIEDL *and* VICKI.
        Then perhaps I'm
        Going to let you . . .
ERNST *and* JOHANN (*shouted*)
        Well?
CILLI, FRIEDL *and* VICKI.
        . . . hold my hand!

HANS, ERNST *and* JOHANN.
        Then we'll take you out to supper
        In the most expensive style.
CILLI, FRIEDL *and* VICKI.
        If you think that you can
        Win me that way
        Then it really won't be
        Worth your while.
HANS, ERNST *and* JOHANN.
        Every thought of love we'll scupper,
        And we'll just resist its thrill.
CILLI, FRIEDL *and* VICKI.
        If you play a game of love
        It's the woman always pays;
ALL SIX.   But at supper, man
        Must settle up the bill!

    (THEY *dance*)

CILLI, FRIEDL *and* VICKI.
        If you play a game of love
        It's the woman always pays;
FRIEDL, VICKI, ERNST *and* JOHANN.
        But at supper, man
        Must settle up—
ALL SIX.   At supper, man
        Must settle up—
        At supper, man
        Must settle up the bill!

(As the music ends, Hans *crosses to the bar where he begins surreptitiously to mix a mysterious cocktail in a shaker.* Cilli *turns to the Waiters and Waitresses)*

Cilli. Now off to your posts, all of you. And when the time comes we're going to show them what it *used* to be like in Vienna!

(Under the direction of Johann *and* Ernst, *the* Waiters *and* Waitresses *disperse.* Hans *fills a glass from the cocktail shaker, and moves down* c *to Cilli)*

Hans *(offering the glass)* Something special for madame.
Cilli. Oh? *(Suspiciously)* And what's so special about it?
Hans. The recipe, madame. I captured it from an Italian prisoner. It had been in his family for years.
Cilli *(taking the glass)* And what do they call it?
Hans. Its name is Veritas.
Cilli. Veritas? *(She takes a sip, and shudders)* Ugh! It tastes more like Sanitas.
Hans. Veritas: the Latin word for truth. Tell an untruth after tasting it and the brain immediately signals its disturbance to the stomach!
Cilli. Pooh! Try a story like that on a child of ten, not on a grown woman of thirty. *(She gives an enormous hiccup, then registers astonishment)*

*(*Hans *laughs)*

Thirty-one. *(Another big hiccup)* All right, then; thirty-five.

*(*Hans *waits tensely for the hiccup; it doesn't come)*

How dared you try this nonsense on *me?*
Hans. Because I wanted to make quite sure about tonight. Is this Nina What's-her-name really coming?
Cilli. Of course she is!

(Again, Hans *waits; but there is no hiccup)*

Hans. And are we going to be able to pay her what she's asking?
Cilli. We certainly are!

(Once more—no hiccup)

Hans, I hate you. *(She hiccups violently)*

*(*Hans *grins affectionately and kisses her)*

All right, so it does work. *(She offers the glass to him)* *You'd* better finish it up, then.
Hans. Oh, let's forget the whole thing. I only wanted to be sure about tonight.
Cilli *(threateningly)* No, no. *Drink it up.*

(Startled at her intensity, Hans *does as he is told)*

I want to be certain about *last* night.

(HANS *looks apprehensive*)

You were out rather late.
HANS. Ah, but you knew where I'd gone.
CILLI. Of course. You were out with the boys.
HANS. That's right. (*He senses that a hiccup is coming, struggles manfully to repress it, but finally fails in a big way*)
CILLI (*accusingly*) Hansi, was it by any chance with the *girls?*
HANS (*confidently*) Girls? Nothing of the sort.

(*It is* CILLI'S *turn to anticipate—but no hiccup comes*)

CILLI. Hansi, was it *a* girl?
HANS. Certainly not. (*He hiccups*)
CILLI. Getting warmer! Who was she, Hansi?
HANS. Do stop, Cilli. I wanted it to be a secret.
CILLI. I'm sure you did. You'd forgotten about Veritas! Who was she?
HANS. She was no-one you know.
CILLI. Well, I didn't expect a hiccup on *that.*
HANS. If you must know, Cilli, I went to see a woman about a dog. (*No hiccup*)
CILLI. You did *what?* What about? Not that I care. (*She hiccups*)
HANS (*getting angry*) You heard me. I went to see a woman about a dog! (*Again no hiccup*)
CILLI. That Veritas must be wearing off. (*She rounds on Hans fiercely*) Now don't try and fool me . . .

(HANS *cowers away and takes shelter behind the bar. At that moment* ERNST *enters through the swing doors* R, *with an amused expression*)

ERNST (*holding the door open*) A lady to see you, sir.
HANS (*emerging from behind the bar*) Thank heaven! Saved by the bell!

(FRÄULEIN GUMP, *from the Kennels, enters* R. *A lady of uncertain age, she is an Austrian parody of the British "doggy type". She carries a small lidded basket, and seems to be in an overwhelming hurry*)

GUMP (*heartily*) Ah, there you are, Mister Hans. (*She turns to Cilli*) And this pretty lady must, of course, be *Missus* Hans. (*She plumps the basket into Cilli's arms*) Happy New Year, my deah! (*She gives Cilli a hearty slap on the back*) Sorry, I must be going. (*She hurries up stage*) I've got another bitch to deliver before midnight! Cheeriho! (*And with a wave, she is gone*)

(HANS *and* ERNST *laugh uproariously.* VICKI, FRIEDL *and a few of the* WAITRESSES *enter* R *to find out what the noise is about.* ERNST *crosses up* C *and sees Fräulein Gump off*)

CILLI (*indignantly*) And what's so funny about that?
HANS. Aren't you going to look at my New Year's present?

(*The other* Girls *gather round as* Cilli *opens the basket and takes out a very cute puppy—if available, a dachsund. Except for* Cilli, *all the* Girls *make adoring noises*)

Cilli (*pretending*) Ugh! A horrid little dog! (*She hiccups violently*) Oh, sweetie! (*She cuddles the puppy close*) Momma's pretty baby; what a darling! She'll be our good luck charm for tonight. (*She carries the puppy off* r *and exits*)

(Vicki, Friedl *and the* Waitresses *follow, all hoping to be next to cuddle the adored puppy.* Ernst *returns from up* c)

Ernst. It looks like being an evening for good luck charms. There's another one coming down the hall right now.

(Ernst *stands to one side as the* Prince *enters*)

Hans. Good evening, Your Highness. I'm delighted to see you. (*He hiccups loudly*)

(Ernst *exits*, r)

Prince (*drily*) I must say you *sound* delighted.
Hans. Take no notice of it. It's just the prevailing wind.
Prince. Is my son here? I understand that this is one of his famous haunts.
Hans. Oh, quite, quite. He's here every night.
Prince (*raising his brows*) *Every* night?
Hans. He is, on the dot. Mind you, he does get every third Tuesday evening off; his union insists on it.
Prince. His union? What the devil are you talking about? Kindly tell him I'd like to speak to him.

(Max *enters from the kitchen*, r. *He is in waiter's costume, and carries a tall pile of plates. At first he cannot see the Prince*)

Hans. *You* tell him, sir. Here he is.

(Max *sets the plates down on a table*)

Prince (*astonished*) Max!
Max (*looking up, coolly*) Hello, Father. (*He brushes past the Prince; plates in hand*) Excuse me, I have to finish my tables.
Prince (*at bursting point*) Finish your tables? What is this nonsense? And what are you doing here dressed up as a confounded waiter?
Max. That's easy enough to answer. I *am* a "confounded waiter". (*He edges past the Prince to another table*) If you don't mind . . . ?
Prince. Good God! When they told me that you were always here I expected to find you amusing yourself at the bar, not making a fool of yourself and disgracing our family name by *working!*
Max. Perhaps I am amusing myself. Perhaps I find working more "amusing" than vegetating in a stuffy palace, trying to pretend that life is still the same as it was in 1914!

Prince (*disgustedly*) Revolutionary poppycock!

(*At the sound of raised voices,* Cilli *enters anxiously, followed by* Ernst *and* Johann)

Max (*coldly*) Call it what you like, Father. You remember Ernst? And Johann? Two of my platoon officers in the Guard?

(Ernst *and* Johann *click their heels instinctively*)

Ernst is our maître d'hotel, Johann is in charge of the wine. When they found themselves on the streets, without even a pension, what did you expect *them* to do? (*Sadly*) You live in the past, in the fool's paradise of 1914. Well, I don't want to go back to that. I'd rather work here, decently, with my old friends.

Prince. Still mooning over that little shop girl?

Max (*deliberately*) No. As a matter of fact I never even think of her. And now perhaps you'll allow me to get on with my work?

Prince (*with a shrug*) Very well, then . . . (*half scornfully, half sadly*) waiter!

(*The* Prince *turns to exit and find himself face to face with Cilli*)

Cilli. And let me tell you something; he's a very *good* waiter.

Prince. Really?

Cilli (*imitating him*) Yes, rahlly!

(*The* Prince *exits up* L, *followed by* Cilli *who makes menacing gestures behind his back.* Ernst *comes impetuously forward as though to console Max.* Max *has turned away.* Johann *restrains Ernst with a headshake and a gesture that silence would be best.* Ernst *and* Johann *exit* R)

"NO MORE"   No. 19

Max.   No more—
              No more those evenings long ago,
              Like footprints in the drifting snow,
              They are, alas, no more.
              No more—reunion in the April rain,
              The magic of a waltz refrain,
              The smile I still adore.
              The dream is done, and tho' I wake,
              I feel its rapture anew.
              For here am I, still deep in love,
              But where, beloved, are you?
              No more—
              Those partings on the brink of day,
              Sweet moments when we used to say
              "Until we meet again".

Each year the spring comes round again
With blossom bright upon the bough,
And April's beauty sweet as pain
Belongs to other lovers now;
That rhapsody in Spring's romantic key
Is lovely still, but never more for me.

No more—
No more the touch of hands that cling,
The music that the gipsies sing,
When there are stars above.
No more—the kisses and the laughter gay
Of that enchanted yesterday
When we were so in love.
No more the thrill of whispered words
Like violins in the night.
The parted lips, the laughing eyes
That made a world of delight.
No more—
The beauty of a dream come true,
The ecstasy of loving you.
That moment so divine,
No more, no more is mine.

(*As the music ends,* CILLI *enters* R, *and* MAX *crosses towards her*)

CILLI (*shaking her head*) Poor Max!

MAX. I'm sorry, Cilli. It takes a couple of royal and ancient Schmettoffs to make a scene like that. Anyway, you won't be troubled with *me* much longer. I've decided to leave Vienna.

CILLI (*tenderly teasing*) Running away, Max? Your father was right. You *do* think of Greta still!

MAX. No, no, that's all finished. I sent her a letter explaining I had been called away. She never answered it. When I came back to look for her she was gone. (*Bitterly*) The dream had ended! Thank you, dear Cilli, for all you and Hans have tried to do for me. I only hope that my successor will be a better waiter . . . and more cheerful company! (*As though to hide his emotion, he breaks away, and exits* R)

(CILLI *stares after him, then begins to chuckle*)

CILLI. He loves her! (*She twirls round the stage, singing*) He loves her! He loves her! He loves her!

(HANS *enters* R, *followed by* ERNST *and* JOHANN *who stare at Cilli's demonstration*)

HANS (*tapping his forehead*) She's gone crackers! (*He follows her around, imitating her*) "He loves her, he loves her, he loves her."

MELOS—ARRIVAL OF THE GUESTS No. 20

(FRIEDL *enters up* L *and runs down to Cilli*)

FRIEDL (*breathless with excitement*) Cilli, stop it! They're beginning to arrive. You never saw such a crowd!

JOHANN (*with a commanding handclap*) Come along, all of you. To your places! This is it!

HANS (*to Cilli*) Here's luck, my darling!

CILLI. And *you* go slow on the bottle.

HANS. What, *me?* I never touch the stuff! (*He feigns a loud hiccup, then crosses to the bar*)

(*As the music crescendoes, extra lighting is built up and the scene becomes one of bustle and excitement. The* WAITERS *enter and take up their posts.* VICKI *enters to the terrace, where she waits to collect the guests' coats.* FRIEDL *goes to the bar and collects the cigarette tray from Hans.* HANS *busies himself with preparations, and* ERNST *dons his ceremonial chain and seizes a leather-bound wine list.* CILLI *goes up to the terrace, where she joins* VICKI, *waiting to welcome the guests. As a climax to this, the first few* GUESTS *begin to arrive, up* L. JOHANN *refers to his order-sheet, bows, and shows them to their tables. More and more* GUESTS *arrive and are greeted and accommodated. Finally, only the extreme down* L *and the extreme up* R *tables are left unoccupied.*

At an agreed cue, the Melos fades—to be replaced by the chatter of the GUESTS. *Then the lights are lowered and spotlights are switched on, focused on the doors,* R)

BALLET: "TYROLEAN LIFE"   No. 21

(*A number of* DANCERS *enter into the spotlights and perform a Tyrolean Novelty routine. During the dance, the general business of a busy restaurant is continued.* ERNST *supervises the serving of wine, while* HANS, *at the bar, makes cocktails which are carried to the tables by the* WAITERS. FRIEDL *serves a few customers with cigarettes and then exits up* R. CILLI *crosses down to the bar, where she stands revelling in the scene. During the Ballet, the* CHORUS *sing*)

CHORUS.   Yodelay, yodeli, yodelay-hiti.
                 Yodelay, yodeli, yodelay-hiti.
                 Yodelay, yodeli, yodelay-hiti.
                 Yodelay, yodeli, yodelay-hiti.
                 Yodelay, yodeli, yodelay-hiti.
                 Yodelay, yodeli, yodelay-hiti.
                 Yodelay, yodeli, yodelay-hiti.
                 Yodelay, yodelay-hiti.

(*The Dance continues. As it reaches its climax, the* CHORUS *again join in*)

                 Yodelay, yodeli, yodelay-hiti.
                 Yodelay, yodeli, yodelay-hiti.
                 Yodelay, yodeli, yodelay-hiti.
                 Yodelay, yodelay-hiti.

Yodelay, yodeli, yodelay-hiti.
Yodelay, yodeli, yodelay-hiti.
Yodelay, yodeli, yodelay-hiti.

(*The* Guests *are now at such a pitch of enthusiasm that the Dancers
end to a wild and continuous accompaniment of yodels, shouts and cheers.
As the Ballet finishes the* Dancers *exit* R *and the* Guests *cheer and
applaud with great gusto.*

During this, Friedl *returns from up* R, *obviously in a state of great
excitement, and crosses towards Cilli.* Hans *pours two drinks, hands one
glass to Cilli and toasts her with the other. Before* Cilli *can drink,* Friedl
reaches her and taps her on the shoulder. Cilli *turns to Friedl, handing her
glass back to Hans. Finding himself with a glass in each hand,* Hans
decides the best thing to do is to drink them both)

Cilli (*to Friedl, impatiently*) Well, well, what is it?
Friedl. Oh, Cilli! Guess who's here! She's just arrived. (*She
whispers in Cilli's ear*)
Cilli. All right then. Bring her in at once. I was expecting her.

TANGO MELOS: "GOOD-NIGHT VIENNA"   No. 21a

(*The orchestra strikes up a reprise of "Good-Night Vienna", played
in strict tango tempo, and a number of guests leave their tables and begin to
dance.* Friedl *hurries away up* R. Cilli *turns to recover her glass, and
registers on finding that Hans has emptied it.* Hans *stares innocently.*
Helga *enters to the terrace from up* R, *followed by* Friedl. Helga *is
superbly dressed and bejewelled, and has a luxurious fur cape.* Vicki
greets her, and takes the cape from her)

Helga (*seeing Cilli, and moving quickly down to her, with hands out-
held*) Cilli!
Cilli. Countess Helga!

(Helga *and* Cilli *embrace.* Ernst *and* Johann *recognize the new
arrival, click their heels and bow.* Vicki *and* Friedl *hover adoringly, and*
Hans *comes forward from behind the bar. At that moment* Herr Gru
enters up L. *He is a fat, pompous man of about fifty. With him is* Mitzi,
a youthful blonde with too-obvious charm. Herr Gru *and* Mitzi *slowly
descend the steps together, and move towards the bar*)

Helga (*looking around her*) How good it is to see you all again.
And what a wonderful party you seem to have arranged!
Johann (*seeing Herr Gru approaching, and nudging Hans*) Ah-hah!
Here comes trouble!
Ernst. Only the *first* instalment.
Hans (*moving quickly to head off Herr Gru*) Ah, Herr Gru. And
Fräulein Mitzi. (*He bows fulsomely to them, then shepherds them towards
the bar, signalling his real feelings to Cilli, behind their backs*) Two large
dry martinis, as usual?

Gru (*slightly offensively*) Do you mean to tell me that you *really* have this Nina Musique singing here tonight?

(Hans *woffles helplessly, and looks to Cilli for assistance*)

Cilli (*intervening hastily*) Of course we do.

(Frau Gru, *a formidable dragon, enters up* l, *hanging on to the arm of her prize-fighter gigolo,* Niki. Frau Gru *and* Niki *descend the steps without, for the moment, noticing Gru and his partner*)

Why else do you suppose everybody who *is* anybody has come along? (*She sees Frau Gru looming up*) Oh, my God! (*Quickly, taking Helga over to the bar*) Countess Helga, may I present Herr Gru? He did very well out of Army boots, during the war.

Gru (*snobbishly impressed*) *Countess* Helga? Delighted, I'm sure! (*He bows and kisses Helga's hand*)

Frau Gru (*sharply*) Adolph!

(Gru *starts back, as though he had been stung*)

Aren't you going to introduce your wife? Gru. Of course, my dear. (*He turns to Helga, rather lamely*) Countess Helga, this is Frau Gru!

Frau Gru (*with an exaggerated curtsy*) Oh, Countess!

Johann (*coming to the rescue, and addressing Herr Gru*) Sir, (*he turns to Frau Gru*) and madame, your table . . .

(*The* Grus *exchange a hurried glance and hesitate*)

Better take it while you can. The cabaret is due to start in a few moments.

(Herr *and* Frau Gru, *still confused, allow themselves to be taken by* Johann *to the table, up* r. *Finding themselves stranded at the bar,* Mitzi *and* Niki *look as if they are about to give the game away*)

Hans (*hastily, to Mitzi and Niki*) You two had better have a drink and get to know each other! (*He serves them with drinks*)

(*The dance music has ended, and the* Guests *return to their tables*)

Cilli (*to Helga*) Thank you for getting me through *that!*

Helga (*who has been amused by the whole situation*) I'd do anything for you, Cilli. Especially tonight!

Cilli (*feelingly*) I wish you could make the speech . . .

(Cilli *is interrupted by a chord from the orchestra. The* Guests *stop chattering*)

Helga (*giving Cilli's arm a squeeze*) Good luck, fellow conspirator!

(Ernst *bows to Helga and leads her to the table down* l, *where* Helga *sits.* Cilli *moves* c)

Cilli. Ladies and gentlemen, the moment has now come for me to introduce to you our guest and entertainer of the evening. The singing star from London, Paris and New York . . . *Miss Nina Musique!*

(*The* Guests *applaud. The spotlights concentrate on the terrace, and the orchestra begins*)

"LAUGH WHILE YOU LOVE IN VIENNA" No. 22

(*After a short introduction,* Greta *is heard singing, offstage*)

Greta (*singing, off*)
    Love reigns in Vienna tonight.

(Greta *enters. In dress, make-up, hair-style and, above all, in her air of assurance, she is very different from the Greta of Acts I and II*)

    Take love while you may,
    For a year and a day.
    We can laugh as we love in Vienna.
    The kiss that you steal
    Leaves no heart-ache to heal
    'Neath the stars up above in Vienna.
    Love! Love!
    Seek with a smile
    Half love,
    Or a love that's worth your while.
    So laugh while you may
    Till the dawn brings the day.
    Love reigns in Vienna tonight!

    This love is but a dream,
    Tho' real it may seem,
    Let's laugh at love and be gay.
    As the summer goes,
    As the Danube flows,
    Love must stray, never stay.
    Two arms that offer bliss
    The lips that we kiss
    And shining eyes we adore
    Sound the call to love
    Tempt us all to love;
    Love's a dream we must dream once more!

(*The* Chorus *now sings the refrain, while* Greta *takes a descant, to* "Ah . . .")

Chorus.   Take love while you may,
    For a year and a day.
    We can laugh as we love in Vienna.
    The kiss that you steal
    Leaves no heart-ache to heal
    'Neath the stars up above in Vienna.

GRETA.   Love!
CHORUS.   Ah . . .
GRETA.   Love!
CHORUS.   Ah . . .
GRETA.   Seek with a smile
CHORUS.   Ah . . .
GRETA.   Half
CHORUS.   Ah . . .
GRETA.   Love,
CHORUS.   Ah . . .
FULL COMPANY.
                    Or a love that's worth your while.
                    So laugh while you may
                    Till the dawn brings the day.
GRETA.   Vienna, my Vienna—
CHORUS (*humming*)
GRETA.   Where the world revolves in waltz-time!
CHORUS.   To the music of a melody gay
FULL COMPANY.
                    Love reigns in Vienna—
GRETA.   —tonight!
FULL COMPANY.
                    Love reigns in Vienna tonight!

(*As the number ends,* GRETA *is given tumultuous applause*)

GUESTS. Encore, encore! More, more!
GRETA (*as soon as she can make herself heard*) Thank you! And, of
course, I am going to sing again for you, if you will first allow me a
moment in which to greet old friends, and recover from the emotion
of being back home again after so many years.

(*Again the* GUESTS *applaud.* CILLI *beckons Greta, and* GRETA *comes
to join Helga at the table down* L. HANS, VICKI, FRIEDL, JOHANN, *and*
ERNST *desert their duties for a moment to surround Greta and welcome her.
The* GUESTS *resume their chatter*)

Hansi! (*She embraces him*)
CILLI (*to Hans*) That's enough of that, my lad. A bottle of champagne for Mam'oiselle Musique, and (*she lowers her voice, pointedly*)
send the special waiter!

(HANS *exits* R)

VICKI. Greta, you were wonderful.
FRIEDL. However did you get here, Greta?
GRETA. It was all Helga's doing. She recognized me at my con-
cert in Paris. And when she told me about you all . . . I suddenly
wanted to come home.
JOHANN. And what have you been doing all this time?
GRETA (*with a shrug*) Oh, changing my name, working, travel-
ling . . . trying to forget.

(MAX *enters* R, *carrying a bottle of champagne in an ice-bucket. He crosses to the table down* L *and hovers behind it, without seeing Greta's face*)

HELGA. And did you succeed?

GRETA (*with assumed casualness*) Oh, yes! (*She pauses, then continues eagerly*) No, of course I didn't. Where is he? What does he look like?

CILLI (*to Max*) Waiter, you may serve the champagne.

(MAX *steps forward and finds himself face to face with Greta. For an instant he registers an amazed reaction, then he recovers his self-control*)

MAX. Champagne, mam'oiselle?

GRETA. Max!

(*Quietly,* VICKI, FRIEDL, JOHANN *and* ERNST *return to their work*)

MAX (*coldly*) This is quite a surprise . . . mam'oiselle.

GRETA. I hoped that I should find you . . .

MAX. I wonder that you troubled.

GRETA (*very hurt*) Max!

MAX. You're so famous now. You must be very busy.

GRETA. Max, what was I to do? You went away without a word . . .

MAX. Without a *word?* I sent you an explanation.

GRETA. I never received it.

MAX. I searched Vienna for you . . .

GRETA. I'd left the city. The shop was closed down . . .

(HELGA *and* CILLI *are becoming increasingly concerned at the turn this reunion is taking*)

MAX (*filling her glass*) Your champagne, mam'oiselle.

GRETA. Thank you, (*she pauses, and then—not unkindly*) waiter. (*She raises her glass*) Here's to the Count, and the Flower Girl—and to the only fairy story that *didn't* end happily ever after! (*She drinks, defiantly*)

CILLI (*unhappily*) Oh, Greta!

GRETA. Don't worry, Cilli. (*She sets down her glass, and rises*) Ladies and gentlemen, would you like another song?

GUESTS. Bravo! She's going to sing again!

GRETA. This time I'm not going to sing anything very famous or grand. Just an old favourite of mine, that used to mean a great deal to me—and to some other people here tonight!

(*The* GUESTS *applaud loudly, as the music begins*)

REPRISE—"MY PRETTY FLOWERS"   No. 23

(GRETA *sings the number with considerable meaning and emotion. During her performance* MAX *finds great difficulty in maintaining his aloofness*)

My pretty flowers will be
A token when we part,
Each coloured flower a word
I've spoken in my heart.
Though petals may fade by morning
Just don't be afraid—
Their warning be scorning.
There'll be a fragrance
You'll remember in the air,
And you'll have roses in December
While you care.
Then one happy day—
I'll take you in my arms and say:
"My pretty flowers have kept you
True to me."

(*As the music ends, there is a brief silence. Before the* GUESTS *can applaud, loud voices can be heard off* R)

WILHELM (*off stage*) Let go of me, I tell you.
HANS (*off stage*) Come on, you. Come on, let's hear all about it.

(GRETA *looks puzzled and put out. The* GUESTS *begin to call for silence angrily.* HANS *enters* R, *frog-marching* WILHELM *ahead of him*)

CILLI (*indignantly*) Hans! (*She darts across to him*) Have you gone out of your mind?
HANS (*the master, for once*) Silence, woman!

(*With a gasp,* CILLI *collapses into the arms of Ernst*)

Well, Count Max, do you recognize him?
MAX (*staring at Wilhelm*) Why, yes. It's Wilhelm—Wilhelm who used to work for my father.
HANS. Exactly. It's (*with a vicious tweak at Wilhelm's ear*) Wilhelm——

(WILHELM *protests violently*)

—sweet William! Now William, tell the Count what Prince Schmettoff did with the letter he left to be delivered to Miss Greta.

(*The* PRINCE *enters up* L. *He is in evening dress. For the moment, he stands unnoticed*)

Well, William, go on! What did His Highness do?

(*The* PRINCE *begins to move down stage*)

WILHELM. He—er—took it and—er . . . (*He sees the Prince and, if possible, looks even more miserable*)
PRINCE. He lit his cigar with it. Wasn't that so, Wilhelm?
WILHELM. Y-yes, Highness. That was so.
GRETA. *What?* You mean that Max really *did* leave a letter for me?

PRINCE (*not recognizing her*) For you, mam'oiselle?

GRETA. Yes, for *me*. Perhaps you don't recognize me, now that I'm no longer "that cheap little flower girl".

PRINCE. You knew this, Helga?

HELGA. Yes. That was why I asked you to be my guest here to-night. (*Reproachfully*) How *could* you have destroyed that letter?

PRINCE. What happened that night was a blow to my pride.

HELGA. Do you imagine that it hadn't been a blow to *mine?* Though I should never have forgiven myself if I had stood in the way of those two, who loved each other so much!

PRINCE (*in a low voice, tensely*) No, Helga? Perhaps *I* have never forgiven myself either. (*He turns to Greta*) If you will accept the humble apology of an old man. And you, too, Max, for the wrong I did to you both. (*He crosses to Greta, takes her hand and places it in Max's*) If my heart's best wishes can be of any recompense to you, you have them.

CILLI (*to Hans*) Oh, my clever little Hansi-Pansi.

HANS. And now, may I have a lovely little drinkie-winkie?

CILLI. Yes, you may but you mustn't get tighty-pighty!

HANS. Get tighty-pighty? I'm going to get stinkie-pinkie!

(*The* GUESTS *all laugh.* MAX *takes* GRETA *in his arms*)

GRETA (*to the Guests at large*) For the benefit of those of you who don't know the whole story, this is a happy ending!

FINALE   No. 24

FULL COMPANY.
>Good-Night, Vienna,
>Where moonlight fills the air with mysteries,
>The world is waiting on the edge of the day,
>Just waiting to say "Good-night,
>Vienna, good-night!"

The CURTAIN *falls*

PROPERTY PLOT

ACT I

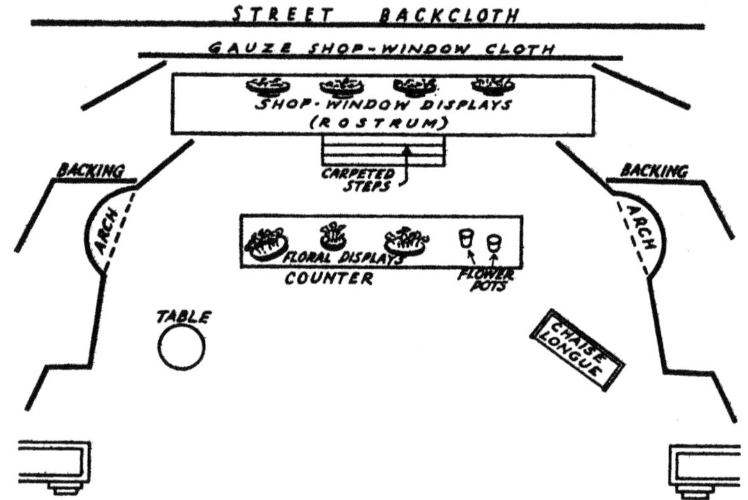

On stage: Counter (below steps, c) *On it:* Flower displays in vases and baskets (in one of the displays, a loose red rosebud *for* Greta *to give to Max*), a tier of flower-pots at l end
Round table (down r) *On it:* order-books and pencils, spools of ribbon, greeting cards, writing materials *Under it:* waste basket
Chaise-longue (down lc)
Dressing: flower arrangements in shop windows, flowers for Assistants with wire, ribbon, twine and wrapping paper for bouquets. Cardboard flower-boxes, ready packed, ribboned and labelled (*to give to* Cilli)

Off stage (l) Cardboard box and damaged carnations (Cilli)
Sunshade (Lea)
Parasol (Ilena)
Military equipment, ad lib. (Hans)
Boxes of wine glasses (Ernst *and* Johann)
Bottles of wine (Officers)

Off stage (r) Telegram (Greta)
Woman's shoe and shoebrush (Hans)

Monocle (PRINCE)
Corkscrew (CILLI)
Sealed envelope containing orders (ORDERLY)
Handbag. *In it:* order for flowers (HELGA)

ACT II

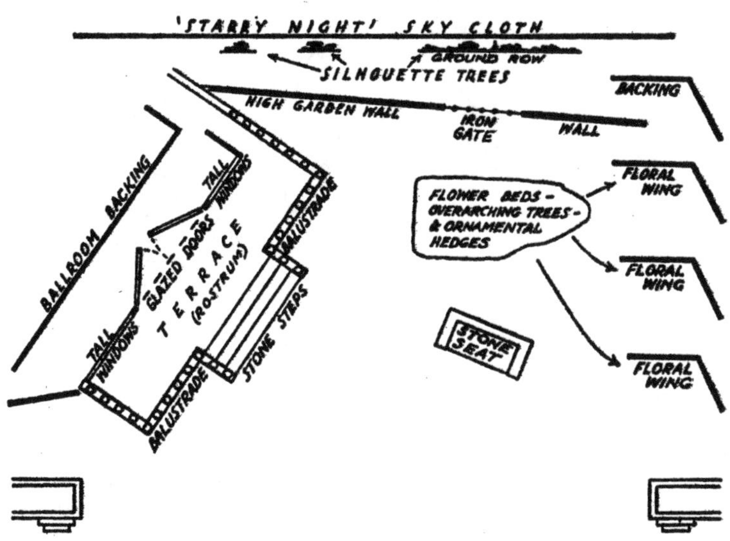

On stage: Stone garden seat (L of C)

Off stage (R)   Tray. *On it:* plate of sandwiches, 5 glasses of champagne
        (HANS)
      Lorgnette (DIPLOMAT'S PARTNER)
      Guest list (WILHELM)
      Jewellery-box. *In it:* ring to fit Helga's finger (PRINCE)
      Envelope (MAX)
      Silver tray. *On it:* cigar-box containing cigars, cigar-cutter,
        flint lighter (WILHELM)

ACT III

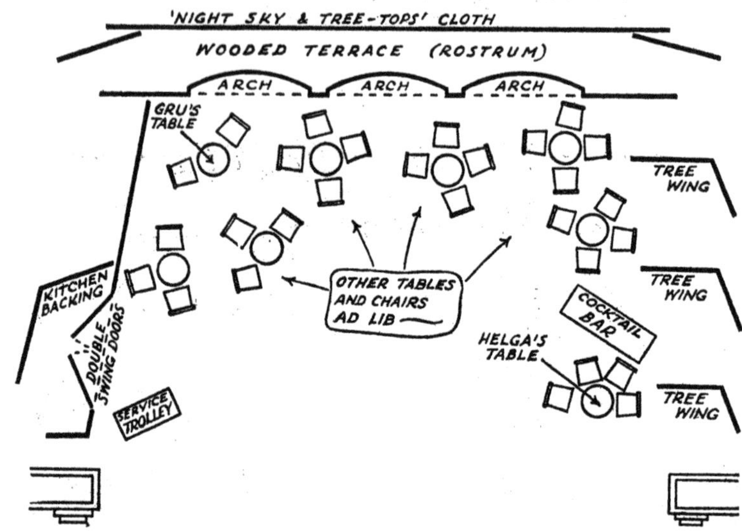

On stage: Cocktail bar (down L) *On it:* bottles ad lib., including brandy, champagne, martini and gin, glasses ad lib., including brandy, champagne and cocktail glasses, cocktail-shaker, dressing ad lib.; telephone, order-book and pencil (*for* JOHANN) *Behind it:* cigarette tray with stock (*for* FRIEDL)

Service trolley (down R) *On it:* telephone with long lead, order-book and pencil, dressing ad lib., including supply of cutlery and glasses (*for* WAITERS *and* WAITRESSES), wine-waiter's chain and leather-bound wine list (*for* ERNST)

Tables and chair (outdoor café style) ad lib.

Off stage (C) Newspaper (CILLI)

Off stage (R) Dog basket. *In it:* dachsund puppy (GUMP)
Pile of plates (MAX)
Order sheet and pencil (JOHANN)
Variety of filled wine bottles (ERNST *and* WAITERS)
Orchids (*for* HERR GRU's *plate*)
Bottle of champagne in ice-bucket (MAX)

BASIC LIGHTING PLOT

ACT I

To open: Shop interior—day. Full lighting
No cues

ACT II

To open: Evening moonlit exterior, with bright light-spill from the ballroom, R
No cues

ACT III

To open:	Night exterior. Café area well lamp-lit	
Cue 1	HANS: "I never touch the stuff?" *Slowly build up general lighting with music crescendo*	(Page 58)
Cue 2	Music fades *Dim general lighting. Bring on spots to focus on doors* R	(Page 58)
Cue 3	DANCERS exit *Return to Cue* 1	(Page 59)
Cue 4	CILLI: "Miss Nina Musique!" *Dim general lighting. Bring on spots to focus on terrace, up* C	(Page 61)
Cue 5	Applause following Music No. 22 *Return to Cue* 1	(Page 62)
Cue 6	"Would you like another song?" *Bring on spots to focus on* GRETA	(Page 63)
Cue 7	End of Music No. 23 *Return to Cue* 1 *Remain to end of play*	(Page 64)

EFFECTS PLOT

ACT I

Cue 1   CILLI and HANS knock over flower-pots   (Page 13)
Crockery crash

Cue 2   CILLI and HANS exit R   (Page 19)
Glass crash, off R

ACT II

Cue 3   CILLI: "Vicki! Friedl!"   (Page 44)
Distant trumpet call
(not in Band Parts)

ACT III

Cue 4   CHORUS (*singing*) "Dear little house in the trees"   (Page 46)
R *telephone rings, in tempo with the music*

Cue 5   CHORUS (*singing*) "Book another table for two"   (Page 47)
L *telephone rings, in tempo with the music*

Cue 6   HANS, ERNST and JOHANN drink   (Page 49)
Pause; then L *telephone rings ad lib., until* JOHANN *lifts the receiver*

Cue 7   JOHANN rings off   (Page 49)
R *telephone rings ad lib., until* ERNST *lifts the receiver*

Cue 8   FRIEDL: "Very funny. Ha-ha!"   (Page 49)
Both telephones ring together, ad lib., until VICKI *and* FRIEDL *lift the receivers*

www.ingramcontent.com/pod-product-compliance
Ingram Content Group UK Ltd.
Pitfield, Milton Keynes, MK11 3LW, UK
UKHW021822150726
7214IPUK00017B/277